HELP! I'm Ruining My Kids

In *Help! I'm Ruining My Kids*, Abbey's writing is raw, honest, relatable, and deeply encouraging. Moms carrying hidden guilt and shame will feel seen and understood, and her unique blend of gospel principles, theology, and science-backed strategies offers both truth and practical tools. Moms in need of a breakthrough will come away with lightbulb moments, a plan to break reactive patterns, and hope for moving forward in both motherhood and personal holiness.

Emily A. Jensen, coauthor of *Risen Motherhood* and *Gospel Mom*

For anyone who's ever felt they aren't the mom they thought they would be, Abbey's words are a healing balm to the disappointed soul. She's given us a rare gift: a book filled with hope that also meets us in our humanity.

Kate Strickler, founder, Naptime Kitchen; author, *I Just Wish I Had a Bigger Kitchen*

In a world overflowing with parenting tips, hacks, and how-tos, *Help! I'm Ruining My Kids* is an anthem of grace-filled dependence on God. Abbey's warm and authentic writing makes you feel like you are sitting at a coffee shop with another in-process mom, gleaning wisdom rooted in God's Word. If you're a mom discouraged because motherhood hasn't looked the way you hoped, this book will meet you right where you are and remind you that the gospel truly transforms not only how we parent but also how we live as beloved children of God.

Gretchen Saffles, bestselling author, *The Well-Watered Woman*

For those of you who know Abbey and her heart for Jesus and motherhood, it will come as no surprise that in her newest book she offers moms the kind of genuine hope everyone is desperate to hear. She does this like a loving friend, full of sincerity and personal compassion. Her words are deeply practical and deeply theological as she points us to Jesus. This book is exactly what every mom needs to hear right now.

Adam Griffin, lead pastor, Eastside Community Church, Dallas, Texas; host, *The Family Discipleship Podcast*; author

Abbey's new book is a refreshing reminder that parenting isn't powered by our perfection but by God's presence, offering freedom, hope, and the assurance that he's at work in our kids' lives, even when we fall short. A wise and theologically grounded guide for weary, overwhelmed moms. Who doesn't need that?

Megan Michelson, director, Birds & Bees

This gospel guide confronts "mom guilt" head-on! Abbey takes raw moments of motherhood and pulls them through the sieve of the gospel and its application. Her writing is filled with truth and tact, and it thrusts moms into the arms of the God we can trust to transform us. You will be left filled with hope, not only in how you see your role as a mom but also in how you see your role as a daughter of God.

Blair Linne, author, *Made to Tremble* and *Yara the Brave and The Swirling Worry*

Abbey's writing is the kind you don't just read—you feel it. Her words are raw and unpretentious, tender yet weighty. And they reach straight into the hidden places of a mother's heart. There's something deeply therapeutic about the way she speaks truth, always wrapped in the language of the gospel. Abbey's vulnerability, honesty, and steadiness shine through every page. This book doesn't shout. It simply tells the truth with courage and clarity, inviting moms to stop hiding and meet grace right where they are. Readers won't walk away the same; they'll walk away lighter, steadier, and more rooted in hope.

Rebekah Hannah, children's ministry director, Redeemer LSQ in NYC; CEO, Anchored Virtual; author, *The Secret to Confidence*

I so wish I would have had this book when I was raising my young children. Abbey would have been a trusted friend and mentor to me, as I longed to be a gospel-rich mom to my daughters. My own kids are now grown, but I heartily commend this book to moms still hard at work shaping the hearts of their kids, even as God shapes theirs. This book is full of both grace *and* truth, real-life stories *and* biblical principles, ideas for application *and* an invitation to rest. It truly is a handbook and companion for every mom who wants to give and receive the gospel in her own heart and home.

Jen Oshman, author; speaker; women's ministry director

A Gospel Guide for the Mom Who's Desperate for Change

Abbey Wedgeworth

ZONDERVAN BOOKS

Help! I'm Ruining My Kids

Published by Zondervan, 3950 Sparks Drive SE, Suite 101, Grand Rapids, MI 49546, USA. Zondervan is a registered trademark of The Zondervan Corporation, L.L.C., a wholly owned subsidiary of HarperCollins Christian Publishing, Inc.

Requests for information should be addressed to customercare@harpercollins.com.

Zondervan titles may be purchased in bulk for educational, business, fundraising, or sales promotional use. For information, please email SpecialMarkets@Zondervan.com.

ISBN 978-0-310-37025-3 (softcover)
ISBN 978-0-310-37027-7 (audio)
ISBN 978-0-310-37026-0 (ebook)

Published in association with Don Gates of the literary agency The Gates Group, www.the-gates-group.com.

HarperCollins Publishers, Macken House, 39/40 Mayor Street Upper, Dublin 1, D01 C9W8, Ireland (https://www.harpercollins.com)

Cover design: Lindy Kasler
Cover photo: Jordan Feeg / Shutterstock
Interior design: Lori Lynch

Printed in the United States of America

25 26 27 28 29 LBC 5 4 3 2 1

For Jamison.

Your friendship is one of God's greatest displays of kindness to me. Thank you for walking with me so closely, for never being surprised, for trusting me with your worst and loving me at mine. Thank you for telling me the truth, encouraging me, celebrating with me, lamenting with me, and consistently reminding me of the gospel. I am so thankful to be walking each other home. Don't you dare get there before me. I can't spare you.

Contents

Foreword

I've known Abbey for a long time, and we have a lot in common. We both have a house full of boys, a love for good theology, and a penchant for writing. But as I read this book, I began to realize just how much more we share.

At a deeper level, we share an attentiveness to mental health in parenting, an awareness of our human limits, and a conviction that embodiment matters—that the way our bodies live and move in the world profoundly shapes the way we parent. In the first four chapters alone, I gained wisdom I didn't know I needed.

As I continued reading, however, the part I was most grateful for was Abbey's honesty. I not only felt like I got to know her, I also encountered someone real. It's easy, especially when writing, to hide your life behind abstractions. Abbey does the opposite. She offers her actual life, with all its gifts and flaws, and invites the reader into it. That kind of honesty is a gift—not only because it makes the book relatable and instructive but because it creates space to see grace at work. In Abbey's stories, we see how Jesus meets us precisely in the gaps between who we are and who we long to be.

This book will continually draw your attention to the ways God is at work in your own story and in the lives of your children. Abbey is relentless about directing our attention toward Jesus.

At the same time, the book offers a wealth of practical wisdom. I was especially grateful for the food analogies that represented various ways to weave Scripture into daily life, the spontaneous prayer suggestions, and the ideas for practicing apology and repair.

But enough from me. I commend this wonderful book to you and pray that the Lord will use it to remind you of his love—and to transform your family through it.

With hope, Justin Whitmel Earley
Founder of Avodah Legal and bestselling author of *Habits of the Household, The Body Teaches the Soul,* and others

Introduction

Desperate for Change

"Mommy is feeling a little frazzled," I confessed, glancing in the rearview mirror at my three boys crammed into an overcrowded row of boosters and car seats. "Can you just not touch or aggravate each other for the rest of this car ride?"

Desperate for quiet, I put on a movie, a treat usually reserved for the last hour of a road trip.

Pressing play, I pleaded, "Just watch this show and be quiet, okay? We're almost home."

Our new puppy lay curled up in the passenger seat, cloaked in wrinkly skin and softly snoring in peaceful oblivion, unaffected by the chaos. Not me. My jaw was tight. My shoulders were tense. My skin felt taut. Trying to take deep breaths, none of which seemed to fill my lungs, I started racking my brain to figure out what was making me so anxious.

A shrill cry interrupted my thoughts. "He pinched me!" my youngest squealed. With all the calm I could muster, I reminded them through gritted teeth, "Boys, please just keep your hands to yourselves and watch the show."

In the few moments of silence that followed, I heard my stomach rumble. The console snack bag was empty. Of course, the ones I packed for me had been devoured by my children. I wanted out of this car. I wanted out of my skin.

Is this what claustrophobia feels like? Just as I thought to roll down the windows, we turned onto our dirt road, but being covered in dust didn't feel like something that might help the situation. *I wish they would just pave*—"Stop it!" The shout of another brother interrupted my thoughts, landing in my ear like a soup can on my big toe. It was the last straw. I slammed on the brakes, launching our puppy from the passenger seat into the glove box and creating a cloud of dust around the car.

I whipped my head around and discovered that I had finally captured the attention of the kids who had been blatantly ignoring my requests for the entire car ride. Having their attention, I launched into a "Why can't you just . . . ?!" speech, coldly rattling off shaming sentence after shaming sentence as the young faces of my captive audience went from stunned to scared. And then they were sobbing. My voice stopped suddenly, the effect of my words finally registering. My ears filled with their crying, my eyes pooled with tears, and my head flooded with shameful thoughts.

"I'm a terrible mom."
"How can I treat my own children this way?"
"One day they'll be telling this story to a therapist, tracing all their issues back to me."

We pulled into the garage, the doors of the car opened, and the boys tumbled out, sniffling. Without any prompting, they hurriedly scattered to their designated places for quiet time. But their compliance didn't feel like a win. *They're afraid of me.* With my ears still ringing and my heart still pounding, I crated the puppy, walked to my room, and fell apart.

This is my story of realizing that I needed to change.

Unfortunately, this story is only one of many others like it. These moments highlighting my need to change have happened all throughout my tenure as a mom—and they still happen.

That's not my favorite story to tell, but it's one I'm compelled to share because if we're going to make any progress on this journey together, you've got to know from the outset: I don't have it all together.

But don't worry, this book isn't at all a case of the blind leading the blind. I've seen the goodness of Jesus and the transforming power of his grace in my motherhood journey, and I want to help you do the same.

I *have* changed. I *am* changing. And I hope I never *stop* seeing a need for change in my life, since the standard of perfection is Jesus, and we won't be like him until he returns. The comfort we moms have on this side of eternity is that Jesus knows our lowly states and doesn't give up on us. He's given us a beautiful new identity to live out of and a miraculous reality to live into. My joy abounds over how God has worked in my life. His peace dispels my guilt and fear when I recall all the places where I've failed and consider the ways I'm still failing. And I hope that as you read this book, you will experience that same joy and peace.

Many of us are not the mothers we thought we would be. We fall short of being the mothers we *want* to be. When our heads hit the pillow, our minds are flooded with thoughts of self-condemnation and fear that we're messing up our kids.

For the past year, every time a mom friend asked me what

I was writing, I'd share the title of this book. Without fail, she would respond with some variation of, "I need to read that ASAP." Sometimes she'd even get tears in her eyes and start divulging specifics.

If you worry about how your sin and shortcomings affect your kids, you're not alone. I'm right there with you, and so is every other mom I know.

We live in a fallen world. Things are not as they should be, and that means neither are you. But the good news is that your story doesn't end there. Christ comes to redeem the narrative, and nothing is beyond redemption—not you, not your experience of motherhood, and not your affected children. You *can* change, and you will, with a bit of help from some tools you'll find in this book and a lot of God's unending grace.

Feeling hopeful enough to come along on this trip? Buckle up (don't mind the Goldfish crumbs and sticky seat belts). Let's take a look at the road map for our journey together.

We will begin by dealing with the guilt and shame you feel by helping you embrace your gospel identity. In part 1, we'll dedicate time to *understanding the mom you are*, reflecting on how God made you, what it means to be human, and how your story and circumstances have shaped you. In part 2, we'll explore *becoming the mom you want to be*. We'll help you decide what you want to change and take a look at God's chosen instruments for spiritual transformation: prayer, Scripture, hardship, and community. In part 3, we'll embrace the truth that change takes time and explore some truths and practical tools for *parenting well as a work in progress*. Specifically, this section will help you let go of the desire for performance and perfection, equip you to repair your relationship with your kids when you blow it, and encourage you to trust God with your kids.

While change is a process, we can't press pause on the work of parenting. As you read this book, you're still in the trenches. So each chapter is followed by a "Parenting Connection" aimed to help you not only to put what you read into practice for your own journey toward personal change but also to immediately incorporate the content of each chapter into your interactions with your kids. My prayer is that these tools will help you feel less helpless and more equipped to love your kids well—even if you still feel a long way away from being the mom you want to be.

And finally, just in case you, like me, can't remember why you walked to the pantry, at the end of each chapter you read, you'll find a little recap called "Believe It for Your Motherhood" followed by a section called "Apply It to Your Parenting." These sections offer quick reminders and refreshers you can easily revisit.

When you close this book, I hope you'll feel more hope-filled and equipped for your own journey of becoming a mom who looks more like Jesus and hopefully hand it to another mom who is also desperate for change. She probably won't be too hard to find. If you can already think of someone, consider inviting her to read along with you right now. Later on, we'll highlight the importance of the role of others as we pursue personal change. But just know that reading this book with another mom or a group of moms can aid your efforts to become more like Jesus. For this reason, I've included questions for group discussion in the back of this book. I hope they'll serve you well.

When you look back on the time you spent engaging with this book, I hope you'll remember it with gratitude, seeing it as a place where God met you in your frustration and despair over motherhood and moved you from helplessness to hope.

Chapter 1

Exchanging Shame for a Gospel Identity

Have you ever seen the movie *Divine Secrets of the Ya-Ya Sisterhood*? The film tells the story of a sisterhood of old friends that conducts an intervention to restore the relationship between one of their members and her daughter. As a teenager, I loved the film for its humor. Lines from the movie became—and remain—a fundamental part of my comedic communication with my sisters. A few nights ago, I rewatched the film for the first time since becoming a mom and found myself crying far more than laughing.

In a particularly gut-wrenching flashback in the film, the mother, Vivi, played by Ashley Judd, is awakened by a coughing daughter. The girl relays the news that her siblings are sick and one "pooped the bed." Vivi rises and goes to her children. She hoists one soiled child into the bathtub, yelling at the oldest daughter to help. As she turns to pick up another, the feverish child immediately vomits all over the front of her nightgown. "We throw up in the toilet!" she shouts as the little one tearfully apologizes. The chaos and intensity of this scene continue to grow.

In the putrid scent of vomit and diarrhea, to the soundtrack of the loud cries and coughs of four children in one small bathroom, Vivi's rage-filled eyes stare at her reflection in a mirror. She slaps a rag on the sink edge, lamenting, "Where is your father! Why do I have to do everything myself?" She then steps backward into a pile of loose stool on discarded pants. As another child retches, she lifts her now shaking hands to cover her ears, squeezes her eyes shut, and shouts, "Shut up! Shut up! Shut up!" Her oldest daughter watches her with wide eyes. There is no resolution to the scene.

Watching this film as a teenager, I remember thinking of this woman as a terrible mother who lacked the patience, selflessness, and kindness that characterize the good moms in Renaissance paintings and children's television shows. But as an adult, I related so acutely to what she was feeling, I had tears streaming down my face.

Can you relate to this movie scene? Overtaken by the moment? Feeling surprised by your own behavior? Wishing your kids had a more competent, loving, stable, selfless mother? Experiencing the unsettling awareness of knowing, even as it happens, the harm you're causing them? Encountering their wide eyes on you in a moment when you just want to disappear so there won't be any witnesses to your brokenness?

If you're like me, that scene reminds you of scenes from your own tenure as a mom—scenes you'd rather fast-forward than relive, scenes you desperately hope your kids will forget rather than recall or, worse, *recount* to their teacher . . . or your mother-in-law.

The act of considering and sitting with moments like these brings a deep awareness that this is not the way it's supposed to be—that *you* are not the way you're supposed to be. And you're absolutely right about that.

Not How It's Supposed to Be

I vividly remember my first "this is not how it's supposed to be" moment as a mom, the moment I realized I wasn't the mother I thought I'd be. I was the world's best babysitter and a coveted camp counselor; I was great with kids. All my friends described me as "maternal." I just assumed motherhood would come naturally.

"Just close your mouth!"

Those are the very loud words that, as they escaped from my mouth, brought the image of the mom I *thought* I would be crashing down. Two weeks into the gig, I was screaming—*screaming* at my *newborn,* who was frantically bobbing at my breast, to just latch already. Even as I blamed him (what was so hard about *eating*?), a profound sense of failure plagued me.

But the problem with my motherhood began long before that moment. Travel back with me to, well, the very beginning. Maria von Trapp would call it a "very good place to start," but for us it's an *essential* place to begin if we're going to rightly understand why things, including you and me, are not the way they're supposed to be.

In the beginning, God created everything. Out of nothing, he made a whole universe. And as an overflow of his love, he made human beings. God gave just one rule to Adam before he made Eve, telling him that they could eat of every tree of the garden, except the tree of "the knowledge of good and evil," which would lead to death (Genesis 2:16–17). The command was there to protect their blissful, anxiety-free, harmonious, fulfilling existence of being naked and unashamed.

But one day, Satan slithered into the equation in the form of a sneaky serpent.

And the next part is as gut-wrenching as the *Ya-Ya Sisterhood* scene.

Desiring to be like God, they ate from the tree. Then, suddenly, they were scrambling around in the garden for something to hide their nakedness—to cover the sudden and overwhelming shame they felt.

All of this is recorded in the Bible under the heading "The Fall," which is biblical shorthand for *everything went to pot*. The perfect party was ruined. The glass shattered, and the shards were everywhere. When God announced the results of their actions, he declared that pain in childbearing would be intensified. As moms today, we experience that pain not only in pushing, periods, and perimenopause, but we also feel it in parenting.

There's no aspect of motherhood that the fall doesn't touch. We are *affected* by the sins of others, we're *afflicted* by the realities of a sin-ridden world, and we are *infected* with an inherited sinful nature, passed down to us like a hereditary disease. As we think about pursuing personal change in motherhood, we've got to approach it holistically—with all three of those things in mind. Still, while our sinful condition is not the *only* thing going on, it's the thing we must deal with first.

The word *sin* makes me instinctively recoil. It's a word I hate to type because I imagine you, like me, probably have a negative association with its use (or abuse).

But when I talk about how your personal sin impacts your motherhood, it isn't as a condemning shout. That's not what you need. You're probably already beating yourself up. No, I'm simply wheeling my chair over closer to where you're seated, reading this book, and I'm compassionately looking you in the eye. And in the same tone that a doctor just tearfully told my dear friend that he has cancer, I'm lowering my voice and letting you know that you're sick. You're sick with sin. We've got to name it. Because if we can't name the disease, we can't treat it. You're sin-sick, my friend. But the good news is, thanks be to God, it's extremely treatable.

A Better Covering

When God detailed the consequences caused by Adam and Eve's disobedience, he also talked about the cure. He told the sneaky serpent,

> I will put enmity
> between you and the woman,
> and between your offspring and hers;
> he will crush your head,
> and you will strike his heel. (Genesis 3:15)

This is the first whisper we hear of the gospel. One day, the seed of the woman would defeat evil and provide the solution for shame. It was clear to Adam and Eve that their shame needed covering, but before God sent them out of the garden, he offered them a *better* covering than the fig leaves they fashioned together, foreshadowing the new clothes he would offer us in Christ Jesus.

Just like Adam and Eve, you and I intuitively reach for "fig leaves" to cover the shame we feel in motherhood. We try to cover it by comparing ourselves with moms who seem worse than us, by trying to do more good for our kids to outweigh the damage, by hosting Pinterest-worthy birthday parties and manufacturing "happy memories" for them, by maintaining the appearance of being "put together" with matching outfits, and by clinging to the accolades we get from others about being "a good mom." But those leaves are flimsy. They won't keep you warm, and they'll come undone at the most inconvenient of times, revealing all that you're trying to keep under wraps. The good news of the gospel is this: God has provided a better covering for you through his Son, Jesus Christ.

Learning to Recognize Shame

To address shame effectively, it's important to understand how it differs from guilt and to recognize the subtle yet powerful ways it influences our thoughts and actions. Shame differs from guilt in that it moves from "I *did* something wrong" to "I *am* what is wrong." How can we recognize when we are operating out of shame? In addition to those thoughts, it shows up as

- depression (I am miserable and unredeemable),
- anger (Stay away from me!),
- withdrawal (I don't belong; I don't want to be seen),
- self-harm (This punishes me and silences the shame for the moment), and
- failure speech (I suck! I'm the worst mom on the planet).[1]

We need to be able to identify shame so we can recognize it when it pops up and deal with it before it negatively impacts how we deal with our kids. Christian counselor Dr. Ed Welch defines shame as "the deep sense that you are unacceptable . . . exposed and humiliated. You are disgraced because you acted less than human, you were treated as if you were less than human, or you were associated with something less than human, and there are witnesses."[2] Often the witnesses to the "less than human" actions we commit are our children. They are the witnesses, and sadly, they are also often the victims. Because of this, shame in motherhood sometimes shows up as suicidal ideation. "Why can't I just be happy and stable for my kids?" becomes "They'd be better off without me." "What's wrong with me that I can't cope?" becomes "I just wish I could disappear." Then we experience compounded shame over our suicidal ideation and lose hope for change, believing, "I'm too broken."

Shame-fueled thoughts and habits are an enemy to progress. Why? Because no amount of negative self-talk, self-punishment, or isolation can produce true and lasting change. That type of transformation happens in the context of compassion, safety, and acceptance. Now, shame can sometimes serve a good purpose: when it drives us to God himself to repent of something that is *actually* sinful, and thereby helps protect us from committing that sin again. But the shame that leads us to withdraw from God and refuse to accept his love *prevents* us from changing because it cuts us off from the love, acceptance, power, and motivation of the only One who has the ability to change us.

The Connection Between What You Do and Who You Believe You Are

For many of us, shame also perpetuates the very behaviors we're ashamed about. First, if we let shame tell us who we are, then it will also tell us how to live. This can lead to cycles of avoidance, perfectionism, or harshness toward others. For example, if our inner monologue is constantly "Shame on me," it won't be long before our dialogue with our children becomes "Shame on you!" The pendulum swings hard from shame to blame, damaging relationships and deepening the cycle of shame.

Shame can also hinder our spiritual progress by leading us to doubt our salvation. Have you ever had these thoughts? "If I were really a Christian, I wouldn't be struggling with the same thing over and over like this," or "If I were really indwelled with the Holy Spirit, I wouldn't keep messing up like this." The danger of this type of thinking is that as long as you doubt your position in Christ (your union with him), you will not reach for the provision of Christ (the grace, love, and acceptance he offers). Jesus is not repulsed by you; rather, as you struggle, he is drawn to you. We never see him disparage contrition in the Gospels. We do, however, see him calling out and criticizing the self-righteous. Experiencing conviction is a good thing. The continual awareness of your struggle with sin, rather than prompting you to question your salvation, should actually serve as *evidence* of your salvation. You are a child of God. Nothing can separate you from his love.

This past Christmas, as I walked into a potluck party for a group my kids were involved with, a box of Uncrustables in tow instead of the homeade holiday themed dish, rather than offering an explanation or trying to justify myself, I held up a peace sign and raised my eyebrows to a friend as I set them on the table. "Christ is my righteousness," we said in unison. You see, I have a bit of a reputation in our community for holding up a peace sign and saying, "Christ is my righteousness," when I face any situation that causes my worth and security to feel fragile, whether its walking into the potluck with Uncrustables or handling a situation with my kids in a way that isn't consistent with the mom I want to be. On any occasion when you might be tempted to identify as a "bad mom," you can practically embrace your gospel identity by claiming Christ's better covering just like this. Your righteousness does not come from how you handle a meltdown in the grocery store, whether the pediatric dentist finds cavities, or whether you can keep the playroom tidy. Christ is your righteousness.

We cannot let our thoughts, our actions, our inaction, the state of our homes, or the behavior of our children tell us who we are. Instead, we need to walk into motherhood with a settled gospel identity. Then, from that place of security, we can assess those things honestly and strategically, dealing with them not as if our worth depends on them but with the grace, wisdom, and confidence of a mom whose worth is firmly established in the unchangeable love of God.

When you feel like you've blown it as a mom, don't confuse your actions with your identity. You can confess what you *did*, without wondering what it means about who you *are*. You are not what you do. You are who God's Word says you are. On this side of heaven, you will always be a sinner—a mom who messes up and needs grace. But you're also already a saint—a mom who has been set apart, made holy, and declared righteous (1 John 1:8–10; Romans 1:7; Ephesians 4:12; 5:3; 1 Peter 2:9). You are a new creation (2 Corinthians 5:17). *That's* the identity God has given you to live out of.

So don't let your "I did . . ." statements become "I am . . ." statements (I *did* a bad thing, therefore I *am* a bad mom). Instead, let your "I am . . ." statements, derived from God's Word, guide what you do, encouraging you to walk in obedience (Colossians 3:1; Ephesians 4:24). When your actions don't match up with what God says about you, don't turn away from him in shame. Instead, turn toward him, *run* toward him with all your mess, knowing he will receive you each and every time with mercy, grace, and—can you believe it?—delight (1 John 1:9; Luke 15:20).

The Remedy for Shame in Motherhood

I find comfort in knowing that the apostle Paul related to the feeling of hating who you are and what you're doing and being desperate to change. In his letter to the Romans, Paul communicates that he's frustrated at his own actions, which he reports are the exact opposite of the good he wants to do. In the end, he concludes, "What a wretched man I am! Who will rescue me from this body that is subject to death?" (Romans 7:24).

As long as we're weighing our good moments against our bad, as long as we're excusing what we're doing, as long as we're soothing ourselves with fig-leafy phrases like "At least you don't . . ." or "You're enough!" or "It's okay! Everybody does it!" then we're not ready to receive what Jesus is offering, which is the hope we desperately need. And that's the hope Paul claims in the very next verse: "Thanks be to God, who delivers me through Jesus Christ our Lord!" (Romans 7:25). That's the answer to his desperate question! And it's the answer to yours and mine as we relive the terrible scenes from our motherhood that we hate to recall. *What a wretched mom I am! Who will rescue me from this version of myself?* Jesus.

You're going to encounter plenty of tools and practical suggestions in this book, but what you need more than you need good advice for motherhood and helpful strategies for change is the good news of the gospel. And here it is: You are probably way more messed up than you would ever dare imagine. You are capable of truly terrible things. But—and that's a *big* but—you're also far more loved than you could ever dare dream, and God can use you for good in ways you would never think possible.[3] This is the message of the "gospel" or the "good news" of Jesus Christ. There is grace to cover every single wrong you have ever done and ever will do. Jesus bore your mistakes and all your shame when he willingly gave up his life so that you wouldn't have to live under the weight of that burdensome guilt—so that you wouldn't have to drag it all around with you as you tote your kids and groceries.

That's the next place Paul goes in his letter to the Romans. He writes, "Therefore, there is now no condemnation for those who are in Christ Jesus" (Romans 8:1). This means that if you're in Christ, you're not on trial. Every wrong thing you have done or ever will do, including every way you have blown it as a mom—it's all forgiven. Nothing can separate you from the love of God for you in Christ Jesus. For every sin Satan throws in front of your face, you can say, "You're right, that is horrible, and it's also completely forgiven. I blew it, but Jesus totally covered it."

As your head hits the pillow at night and your own thoughts condemn you, as you weigh the evidence to determine whether you're guilty of being a bad mom, as you imagine the verdict your children will give you as grown adults, you can interrupt those thoughts by imagining the sound of the gavel of the judge of all the earth (who has way more of a right to judge than you do, by the way), banging to declare, finally and irrevocably, that you are not a "bad" mom. He declares you a *forgiven* mom, a *loved* mom, a *fully accepted* mom. And there is nothing, *nothing* you can do to change that. For all that you feel is at stake—your reputation, your sense of self, the well-being of your kids now and in the future, and even your access to *their* kids as a grandmother—here's what isn't at stake: your standing with God. That is what tells you who you are, whose you are. And that, my friend, is the truest and most important thing about you.

Considering the impact of your sin on your kids can make changing feel like an emergency—and perhaps even makes this gospel recap feel like a waste of time. But reflecting on these truths is the best use of your time because the grace that saves you is the grace that changes you.

Take a break from trying to get it together and let that reality sink down into the darkest, most sorrowful, and most guilt-ridden corners of your heart: Even in your ugliest moments of motherhood, the Lord rejoices over you with singing, regarding you as righteous because of the blood of his Son and not because of anything you have or haven't done. *That* is the good news of the gospel—and understanding, embracing, and resting in it is what will lead to true and lasting change in your motherhood (Titus 1:1).

Mothering as a Loved Child Versus as an Orphan

When one of my boys was still in the church nursery, the director called me the day after women's Bible study to let me know that when my son came back the next week, he needed to be in "proper attire." Instantly, my stomach dropped and my chest erupted in heat. It might as well have been social services calling. When I'd dropped him off without shoes the day before, I'd explained that when I told my kids, "Socks, shoes, jackets, and buckle!" on the way out the door, the three-year-old clearly had decided to just do the "socks and buckle" part. But the nursery workers were upset that his being without shoes meant they couldn't take the kids outside as a group. When I had dropped him off, I felt fine. Now, getting this phone call, I felt anything but fine. I felt like a failure. I felt condemned, misunderstood, alone, discouraged, and defeated.

To protect myself from those feelings, I reached for defensiveness. My internal dialogue accused my church of a lack of gratitude for my serving as the interim children's director unpaid for six months. I felt critical of the way this was being handled—I was on my way to a funeral, for crying out loud! Couldn't they have waited until tomorrow? Or for a third, or even a second, offense before hitting me when I was already emotionally vulnerable? I started to compare myself with other less responsible and attentive moms.

And then God's Spirit stopped me with the words of the Son: "I will not leave you as orphans" (John 14:18).

Those words reframed the whole experience for me.

Priest and professor Henri Nouwen articulated that living like someone who is adopted and a loved child of God requires "[pulling] the truth revealed to me from above down into the ordinariness of what I am, in fact, thinking of, talking about, and doing from hour to hour."[4]

As moms, we know this hour-by-hour ordinariness: folding clothes, packing lunches, facilitating reconciliation after sibling squabbles, pulling a screaming child close even though the sound is killing our ears, patiently enduring first-grade reading assignments, emptying the dishwasher, guiding our kids through chore charts, and driving them to soccer practice. Our adoption has profound implications for the way we experience all these moments.

Recalling that relational idea in the moment moved me from a place of feeling defensive and self-protective to resting in the love, total acceptance, and finished work of Jesus. Reminded that I had nothing to prove, I was able to accept this correction from a place of security instead of fighting that correction to feel secure. I proposed that I would start keeping a pair of shoes in the car. When we hung up, I called a friend to help reinforce the truth since my nervous system was triggered, still functioning in shame. Then I spent time in prayer.

The next time I said, "Socks, shoes, jackets, and buckle!" I didn't scream at my kids as if my security rested on their ability to carry out these commands ("Shame on me" did not become "Shame on you"). But I did double-check that everyone had shoes before we left.

By God's grace, I was able to separate this isolated event from my identity as a mom because of my secure identity as a loved child of God. Assurance of my adoption freed me to love my littlest neighbors from a place of security instead of depending on them as my source of security.

Consider the characteristics of an "orphaned" mother in the following table. Put a check mark by the tendencies you recognize in yourself when you have forgotten whose you are. Underline the phrases or words in the "Adopted/Beloved" column that you most want to embrace and embody.

Mom with an Orphan Mindset	Mom Who Knows She Is Adopted/Beloved
Anxious over felt needs: relationships, money, health. "I'm alone and nobody cares."	Trusts the Father and has a growing confidence in his loving care, leading her to worry less.
Lives on a succeed-or-fail basis. Needs to "look good" and "be right." Is performance oriented.	Is learning to live in daily, conscious partnership with God. Is not fearful.
Feels condemned, guilty, unworthy before God and others.	Feels loved, forgiven, and totally accepted because Christ's merit clothes her.
Parents under a sense of unlimited obligation. Tries too hard to please. Burns out.	Feels freed to serve under God's grace. Is steadfast in service. Fueled by God's unwavering favor.
Defensive. Can't listen well or receive feedback on parenting. Bristles at the charge of being self-righteous.	Open to criticism since she consciously stands in Christ's perfection, not her own. Willing to examine herself and eager to grow.

Mom with an Orphan Mindset	Mom Who Knows She Is Adopted/ Beloved
Needs to be right. Idolizes safety and security. Unwilling to fail. Unable to tolerate criticism. Can only "handle" praise.	Able to take risks and even fail since her righteousness is in Christ. Needs no "record" to boast in, protect, or defend. Doesn't force kids to perform.
Excessively self-confident and self-loathing. Discouraged by her kids' behavior. Defeated by her own. Lacks spiritual power.	Confident in Christ and encouraged because of the Holy Spirit's work in her.
Relies only on her gifts to get by in motherhood. Panics when the needs of her kids exceed her know-how.	Trusts less in self and more in the Holy Spirit—a daily, conscious reliance. Asks God for help and wisdom.
Tends to be ungrateful. Has a critical spirit toward her children and her husband. Tears them down.	Relies on the Holy Spirit to guide her tongue. Praises, encourages, edifies, and gives thanks.
Tends to compare herself with other moms, leading to either pride or depression.	Stands confidently in Christ. Her self-worth comes from Jesus's righteousness, not her parenting.
Boasts. Takes credit for her kids' accomplishments and points out her own for fear that someone might overlook them.	Finds that Jesus is more and more the subject of her conversation. She boasts in her weakness as a mom.
Relatively prayerless. Prayer is a last resort. Prays sometimes in public, seldom in private.	Prayer is a vital part of the day, not confined to a quiet time. Loves to talk to the Father.

This chart was adapted from the diagram "Orphans or Children of God" from World Harvest Mission, *Sonship Manual*, 2nd ed. (Jenkintown, PA: World Harvest Mission, 2002), 22.

The apostle Paul writes, "The Spirit you received does not make you slaves, so that you live in fear again; rather, the Spirit you received brought about your adoption to sonship. And by him we cry, 'Abba, Father'" (Romans 8:15). The Spirit of adoption we receive isn't just a nice idea; the Spirit is a living person who reminds us whose we are and empowers us to live as God's children as we raise ours. If you want to live into the reality of who you are in Christ, then you must keep those truths ever before you. Ask yourself as you go through your day, "How might I respond if I fully believed that I am righteous in Christ, loved by God, and indwelled with his Spirit?" And why don't you go ahead and put a few sticky notes on your dashboard, on your bathroom mirror, and beside your kitchen sink to help you remember this.

You are righteous in Christ, loved by God, and indwelled with his Spirit. Parent today like it's true.

The Most Important Work of Changing Is Believing

When people asked Jesus what they must do to accomplish the work God requires, Jesus replied, "The work of God is this: to believe in the one he has sent" (John 6:29). The most important work you have to do as a mom today is *believing* God—placing your faith in the finished work of Jesus. Grace is the horse that has to pull this "change" cart, the wind that has to fill your sails, the battery that's going to power the engine of this vehicle you're driving on your journey to becoming a more Christlike mom.

Every occasion that you feel mom-guilt is an invitation to believe, an opportunity to "refuel," a chance to pause and consider the fullness of the grace you've been shown in Christ Jesus. True, lasting grace-fueled change requires repeatedly rehearsing and reinforcing this truth. Living holy lives isn't just about inhabiting a new positional status; it's operating out of that *relational* reality. You are an adopted, redeemed, fully accepted, and fiercely loved child of God. This is the context in which you parent your kids.

The safety we gain in God's love for us in Jesus gives us the courage we need to take an honest look at our behavior instead of fast-forwarding it, justifying it, or pretending like it's "not so bad." The identity shift of being loved children under grace makes us secure enough to look inside and honestly assess the icky stuff we find in our hearts. And it's vital that we really let ourselves see it. The more appalling your sin is to you, the more outrageous grace will seem. And the more outrageous it seems, the more grateful you'll be for it. And the more grateful you are for grace, the more you'll become like Jesus.

If you were standing in front of me, tearfully recounting your own *Ya-Ya Sisterhood* scene, and I were to pat your shoulder and say, "There, there, things aren't as desperate as they seem," I would be doing you a great disservice. That would only hinder what we're trying to accomplish here. You see, to change, you *have* to be desperate. The question is, are you desperate *enough*? Are you desperate enough to let go of all the ways you've been trying to do it on your own, all the fig leaves you've tried to cover yourself with, all the performance scale-balancing you've been doing to try to soothe yourself?

If you're willing to let go of trying to do mothering all on your own, if you're ready to receive grace, and if you're resting in the secure love of Jesus, then we're ready to begin. We're ready to take a look at what needs to change.

Parenting Connection

We can only experience true and lasting change in the context of grace. The same is true for our kids. Parenting with grace means resting in God's unmerited favor toward us and communicating that unmerited favor to our kids. Now, I am not always happy with my kids' behavior, and it's important that they know this so they can learn right from wrong and cultivate wisdom. But it is also essential that they know they do not fall out of favor with me when they fail. My love and my posture of being *for them* are always theirs.

We have a little refrain to reinforce that concept.[5] When my kids do something wrong, after addressing it, I'll ask them, "Is there any bad thing you could ever do that would make me love you less?" Or I might be more specific.

> "Is there any lie you could tell . . . "
> "Is there any unkind thing you could ever say . . ."
> "Is there any item you could ever steal . . ."

I've assured them that the answer is always no. So when they say no, I ask them, "Why do I love you?" And they know to say, "Because I'm your child." Then I add, "And that's why God loves his children too, even more than Mama does."

But beyond being assured that they can't *lose* my love, I also want my kids to know they can't earn it since grace is, after all, *unmerited* favor. And so we practice the reversal of the same liturgy when they do something excellent or praiseworthy. "Is there any good thing you could ever do that would make me love you more?"

Again, sometimes I'm more specific:

"Is there any number of goals you could score . . ."

"Is there any amount of cleaning you could do . . ."

"Is there any good grade you could get . . ."

When I correct my kids, I reference God's grace, which protects them from shame. When I praise them, I praise God too, for his enabling grace. This language reframes my kids' successes and failures. It frees them from fragile pride, which only produces pressure, and turns it into praise, which frees them from the fear of failure.

Believe It for Your Motherhood

Every wrong thing you have done or ever will do, including every way you have blown it as a mom—it's all forgiven. Nothing can separate you from the love of God for you in Christ Jesus. The first step on your change journey, and every time you see your sin or your shortcomings, is to believe.

Because you are his sons, God sent the Spirit of his Son into our hearts, the Spirit who calls out, "Abba, Father." So you are no longer a slave, but God's child; and since you are his child, God has made you also an heir.

—Galatians 4:6–7

Apply It to Your Parenting

Regularly rehearse the language of grace, or unmerited favor, with your kids.

Q. "Is there any good thing you could do that would make me love you more?"

A. "No."

Q. "Is there any bad thing you could do that would make me love you less?"

A. "No."

Q. "Why do I love you?"

A. "Because I am your child."

Q. "And who else loves you like that, but even greater?"

A. "God."

Part 1

Understanding the Mom You Are

Chapter 2

Living Within Your Limits

Step, step, push. Dangling from the swing, my feet kicked the ground under the large oak tree in our backyard. After I had spent twenty minutes swinging back and forth, the baby in my arms was finally asleep . . . until a sudden onslaught of the sound of cicadas woke him again. My own voice joined the cacophony created by the chorus of baby and bugs, most of the words of "His Mercy Is More" catching in my throat as tears streamed down my face. I was desperate for this day to be over. I wished I could somehow crawl out of the skin I was wearing and be somewhere else, maybe even some*one* else—someone who hadn't just lived this hellish version of bedtime with an infant, a two-year-old, and a five-year-old.

What was it that had pushed me over the edge? My bigger kids splashing water out of the bathtub? My two-year-old running around instead of coming to put on his Pull-Up like I asked? The shrill sound of their persistent laughter as I begged them to be quiet while trying to nurse the baby to sleep? I couldn't remember the last straw, but what I couldn't forget was the sound of my voice or the look on their faces when I snapped.

The baby started screaming around the same time I did, barking at my two older kids, who shared a room at that point, that this day was over. "No books, no snuggles, no anything!" I declared before our real routine even began. With a proclamation that I was done with bedtime and didn't want to hear another peep out of them, I slammed the door to their bedroom and then the porch door too. As I tried to soothe my infant, I wondered if the reason for his inconsolable crying was overstimulation or even pain . . . perhaps because his mama, in her rage, had burst his little eardrum.

Earlier that evening, I had told my husband to go ahead and attend an evening event, that I could handle bedtime solo. But the reality was that I, much like the baby, was exhausted and overstimulated, and I could not, in fact, handle it.

Bedtime was tricky at this point because the baby needed to nurse during the exact window that my two older boys needed a lot of hands-on help and continuous supervision. Not to mention that we had just moved into a home we weren't quite finished remodeling and there were boxes and tools and dust everywhere (you know, the ideal place to have three boys under five). Although it was hard to do it all on my own, I was convinced I *should* be able to do it all alone. I desperately wanted my husband to see me as competent instead of burdensome.

That night, I overestimated my capacity in a season when I was operating on limited sleep, struggling with my inability to exercise (hello, prolapse), feeling overwhelmed by a lot of change and a lack of support, and suffering from what I honestly believe bordered on postpartum psychosis (more on that later). But rather than receiving those limits in humility and asking for help, I hid them in pride, which quickly morphed into shame.

I was singing the words of that hymn as much to myself as to the baby in my arms.

> Stronger than darkness, new every morn
> Our sins they are many, his mercy is more[1]

The gospel was a comfort to me as I recalled it and repented. But I didn't just need to receive God's conviction and mercy for my sin; I also needed his compassion and grace for the human limitations I was so ashamed of.

After that point, my husband and I had a conversation and agreed that from then on, until I was sleeping more and in a healthier mental state, he wouldn't leave me alone with the kids at bedtime unless I had a friend or a sitter with me. This was an act of both repentance and resignation for me, turning from pride and self-sufficiency and, in humility, embracing my humanity.

For the next few months, every time I had to ask for help, I fought embarrassment. And every time my inability inconvenienced my husband, I wrestled with guilt and shame. But I had a choice: Feign capability or be kind to my kids. The godly choice, however humiliating it felt, was to acknowledge my limits for the sake of my children and the glory of God.

Mortal Motherhood: Embracing Humanity

The expression "I'm only human" is a little like nails on a chalkboard for me. People often use their humanity as a justification for harmful but preventable behavior. It feels like an excuse. And if I make excuses, I'll never change, right? In reality, learning to embrace our human limitations is a key part of Christian growth and flourishing. Our limitations are not an *excuse* for poor behavior but an *explanation* for why we don't always feel fully in control of our actions. Understanding and faithfully living within our limits is an important discipline to cultivate if we want to be the mothers God calls us to be.

The whole point of this book is to hold out hope that you *can* change and offer you help to do it. But there are some things that you *cannot* change—namely, your humanity. You and I will always need air, food, drink, and sleep to live and function. God designed us as needy and dependent creatures and called us very good (Genesis 1:31). When Jesus took on flesh, he affirmed that humanity itself is nothing to be ashamed of. By wrapping himself in skin, subjecting himself to hunger and thirst and the need for rest, and *still* remaining sinless, he demonstrated the clear difference between human limits and sinful failure.

I love how Professor Kelly Kapic highlights the implications of the humanity of Jesus as we assess our own humanity, saying, "The doctrine that the Word became flesh . . . liberates us from apologizing for our creaturely limitations. . . . We must not apologize for what the Son of God freely embraces."[2]

In his letter to the Philippians, the apostle Paul invites believers to have the mind of Christ, who didn't count equality with God a thing to be grasped but humbled himself (Philippians 2:5–8). But all too often, as moms, we behave as if equality with God *is* a thing to be grasped. Resenting our humanity, we disregard it and try to rise above it, denying ourselves the very things we need to function well and hiding our needs from others rather than asking for help. We ignore hunger cues, push through when our nervous systems need us to press pause, commit to things we don't have time for, and stay up late watching Netflix, knowing it will impact our capacity to handle the needs of the morning when our kids wake up. We end up overwhelmed and overextended, far from acting like the moms we want to be. And it's often our kids who pay the price.

Bumping up against our limits provides us with an occasion to worship and depend on a God who is limitless. God did not give your kids to an omniscient mom. However it may seem, there is no mom or parenting expert who knows everything. When the needs of our kids exceed our know-how, we are to run to God for wisdom, which he offers generously and without finding fault (James 1:5). When you have to miss the event of one child to attend an appointment with another, you can worship God as the one who is always and everywhere present. When you can't fix a situation or feel powerless to help your child, it drives you from self-sufficiency to a posture of dependence on a God who is always in control.

Our limits are a part of God's design for our good. To be the mom God created you to be, you must embrace his design for you and live within your limits.

Receiving God's Compassion and Help

When I told my friend Julie about admitting that I could not, in fact, handle bedtime on my own, she remarked, "We get it backward: We *resent* our weakness and *excuse* our sin. We should *hate* our sin and *embrace* our weakness." If you want to be a more Christlike mom, you've got to hate falling short of *God's* standards more than falling short of the standards you set for yourself as a mom.

A few years ago, I experienced this firsthand when signing up for rec soccer. The computer stalled when I clicked "Pay." As the page loaded, one of my boys called my name and I walked away from my laptop. Later, I checked "register for rec soccer" off my to-do list. A few weeks later, I called the rec center to see why I hadn't received an email from my child's coach. They informed me that he wasn't registered. Though I begged them to let my son on a team as an add-on, they told me uniforms had been ordered and there was nothing they could do.

This was not a moral failure. This was a human error. I forgot. I blew it. There was nothing to repent of, but I did need to explain my error to my son, apologizing for what it had cost him.[3] To do this, I first needed to humble myself and receive God's compassion and grace for my forgetfulness. Rather than beating myself up, blaming my kids for their constant interruptions, or shaming them for their entitlement concerning activities, my understanding of human limits enabled me to use this experience as an opportunity to talk to my kids about being gracious with ourselves and one another as human beings.

Being tired, overstimulated, hungry, and forgetful are all examples of human limitations. We don't have to feel ashamed about those things. They might create an opportunity for moral failures to show up, but they are *not* moral failures themselves; they are indicators of our *need* for sleep, food, and margin (or maybe a sticky note). Your human limitations and needs are not a reason to hate or berate yourself.

We need to pay attention to our God-given limits and respond to our needs with compassion, the way a mother might respond to the hunger cues of her child. Even if the action that made you aware of your need was sinful and needs to be repented of, that doesn't disqualify you from receiving God's care and compassion. For example, when you blow up at your kids, exposing your utter exhaustion, you can respond to that evidence of fatigue with compassion by asking for help or getting some rest. We can receive *both* God's conviction over our parenting failures *and* his compassion for our frailty as human mothers. One does not require us to abandon the other. The work you're doing is really hard work, and God knows that you were formed as a human being with creaturely limitations (Psalm 103:14). He has compassion for you. Don't withhold it from yourself.

Aiming for Agency

"I think we need to figure out how we can get you some sleep, Abbey."

That's how my therapist responded when I told her the story I told you in the introduction to this book. We'd opted for that poor puppy since we weren't planning to have another baby, but much like a newborn, it was still up in the night every two hours, and your girl was exhausted.

Rather than asking probing questions, she recommended rest because she knew I needed sleep to calm my nervous system and enable my brain to think clearly. The heart work I needed to do couldn't happen until I established an equilibrium.

The same is true for you. Considering your limits may sound like it's an alternative to aiming for heart change, but it's actually an avenue to it. To rewire our brains as God reorders our affections, we need to be in a regulated state. That helps us to maintain the self-control and presence of mind we need to effectively fight sin.

Our agency, or "the feeling of control over actions and their consequences" or "the power and capability to exert [the kind] of influence" that we want to have and that God asks us to have, is directly affected by how much stimulation, sleep, exercise, and nourishment we get.[4] Those things affect our stamina and brain function. This means that one way we combat sin is by pursuing agency.

Perhaps you've been taught that focusing on your own needs is selfish, or that depending on anything but Jesus shows a lack of faith, but living within our limits and caring for our bodies and minds are two of the ways we fulfill the mandate to be sober-minded and resist temptation (1 Peter 5:8–9).

Assessing Your Needs

How do you determine what your needs are? Doctors, psychologists, and neuroscientists can be helpful here. Human beings *need* water, food, oxygen, and a functioning nervous system (which requires sleep) to survive. But you picked up this book because you don't just want to stay alive; you want to live *well*—to be the best version of yourself so that you can have a positive impact on your children. Some of us feel like we can't say we *need* anything other than Jesus. This is true when it comes to our salvation. But Jesus himself acknowledged and provided for the physical needs of people around him.

In Mark 8, Jesus refused to send the crowds home without feeding them because he thought they might faint on the way (v. 3). He did declare himself the Bread of Life, but he also gave them bread for their stomachs. Jesus said, "Man shall not live on bread alone" (Matthew 4:4), and yet God rained down manna for his hungry people (Exodus 16:11–16). So let's take a cue from Scripture and honor our Creator by looking a little deeper at the way he created us. What do we need not just to live but to live well according to his good design?

One tool I have found extremely helpful is the Healthy Mind

Platter. Dr. Dan Siegel and Dr. David Rock designed it as an instrument to help you thrive by identifying seven daily activities that "make up the full set of 'mental nutrients' that your brain needs to function at its best."[5] Consider the elements in the following table. Are you giving your mind everything it needs to function optimally so that you can show up for your kids as the most self-controlled, sober-minded, Spirit-led (instead of reactive) version of yourself?

In seasons when getting all these mental nutrients feels challenging, I delete social media. In the four minutes I would have spent

The Healthy Mind Platter

Mental Nutrients	How much of this am I getting?	What does or what could this look like for me?	What steps could I take to pursue this?
Sleep time			
Physical time (moving your body)			
Focus time (time with a specific goal)			
Time in (quiet reflection)			
Downtime (time with no goal)			
Playtime (creativity)			
Connecting time			

scrolling, I can call a friend because I need connection to thrive, or I can take some downtime by stepping outside to hear the birds sing and take in the beauty of creation. My faith isn't in that phone call or downtime, as if it were a vending machine that would make me kind to my kids. But calling that friend or leaving that space is an act of faithfulness to God because his Word tells me, and modern neuroscience affirms, that if I am to thrive, I need authentic human connection and space to simply breathe.

We bring God glory when we live in submission to the way he designed our brains. We prepare to love our neighbors well when we care for the vessels that do the loving—not at the expense of those neighbors (as some self-care advocates might advise) but for their good, not for our own sakes but for God's glory.

Circumstantial and Seasonal Limitations

Try as we may, in some circumstances and seasons, we are unable to get all the items on the Healthy Mind Platter. For example, in a season with a newborn baby, it's not realistic to expect to get eight hours of uninterrupted sleep. In these seasons, we need to adjust our expectations and ask for extra support or reduce the weight of the loads we carry. If we don't, and instead attempt to push through these limitations, like an athlete overexerting themselves during an injury, it often makes things worse instead of better. If you sprain your ankle, you don't go for a run; you use crutches to give it time to heal. But the expectations we have for ourselves as moms often lead us to despise those limitations rather than humbly adjusting to accommodate them.

Motherhood is never stagnant. Our kids' needs change as they grow, and the amount of sleep and downtime we get fluctuates. We must continually assess and reevaluate our limits in light of our changing circumstances.

Sometimes the demands of my husband's job have limited me in ways that I have resented, like having to find childcare to attend showers or daytime events on Saturdays. Whether it's breastfeeding a baby that won't take a bottle, healing after delivery, or needing to keep a nap schedule for a younger kid, I've found it helpful to meet negative feelings about those limits with the words of Psalm 16:6–7, which says,

> The boundary lines have fallen for me in pleasant places;
> surely I have a delightful inheritance.
> I will praise the LORD.

Our loving Father is sovereign over the limits our circumstances place on us. They are not a surprise to him. When we remember God's sovereignty over our seasons, we are more likely to look for his provision and for his purposes within them. When you start to feel constrained by those "boundary lines," join the psalmist in praising the Lord. When you bump up against new or increased limits, pause and praise him for his limitlessness. Rather than blowing past those situational constraints, learn to live within them, all for the sake of pursuing holiness. Limits help us feel our need for God, and that's a good thing.

If we fail to acknowledge how our circumstances influence our needs and abilities, we will not be able to change. Whether we floor it through those fence lines because we resent them or behave as if they don't exist because of our pride, ignoring them will prevent us from becoming the self-controlled, intentional moms we long to be. Once you recognize the effects of your circumstances, you're responsible to adjust what you can and ask for help for what you can't. And that sort of humility, believing you can't do it all on your own, is an essential first step toward change.

Discerning Your Limitations

To determine your personal and seasonal limitations, begin with the Healthy Mind Platter, then enlist the help of wise mentors and friends to take an inventory of your life. Ask them if there is any way they see you living beyond your limits. As we discuss discerning your personal limitations, I must caution you against using the capacity of others (moms or otherwise) as your metric. Comparison has rarely been helpful for me in this regard but has often been damaging. During that season of hard bedtimes, I remember wondering why what seemed so hard for me seemed so easy for other moms. But God asks each of us to love him with all of *our* heart, soul, mind, and strength, not with the brain and body we *wish* we had or the circumstances that other people have, but with who *we* are and with what *we* have.

So what are *your* limitations? Take a moment to make three columns to list your personal limitations (sleep needs, nutritional needs, etc.), your seasonal limitations (newborn, potty training, etc.), and your external limitations (spousal availability, job requirements, time commitments, etc.).

My Bible teacher friend Chris Gordon once bravely shared with a large group of women that one of her limits is that she needs eight and a half hours of sleep every night. So, she wisely declared, if she wants to address her struggle with anger or depression, she must begin by getting eight and a half hours of sleep as an act of worship, acknowledging that she is not God. She will turn off Netflix and go to bed instead of watching one more episode because she knows what her brain needs to have the most control over what she says, does, thinks, and believes.

Walking It Back

Ironically, our failures can also help us determine our personal limits. Let's do a little workshop, shall we? We will get deeper, I promise, but this is where I'm asking you to start. Think about the last time you lashed out against your kids or noticed your sin negatively affecting them.

Where were you?
What were the circumstances surrounding that event?
Were you hungry?
Sleep deprived?
On your phone?
Had you moved your body that day? Or the day before?
Had you just seen something on Instagram that made you anxious?

The answers to these questions can sometimes reveal unmet needs. If you see a pattern of unmet needs, make a plan to address those. Figure out how much sleep your body needs to feel rested, then establish a bedtime and wake time to give your body the sleep it needs. Find out how often and how much you need to eat (and possibly specific foods) to meet your nutritional needs, then feed your body accordingly. In certain seasons, I have found myself unintentionally sacrificing the mom I want to be on the altar of pursuing the body I'd like to have. Loving your littlest neighbors is a biblical command. Restoring your body to its prebaby size and shape is not.[6] When you sin against your kids, walk it back to discover what led you there. Make the changes and ask for the help you need to maintain agency and avoid temptation.

Move the Chair

When I was still nighttime nursing my firstborn son, I had to walk down a long hallway and turn a corner to get to the nursery. On the inside of this turn was a chair. Night after night, as I rounded that corner, my left quad would ram into it. Each night, I would go to bed thinking, "I'm not going to hit that chair tonight," and yet every night, without fail, I would run into it.

One morning, my husband expressed concern about the bruises all over my thigh. When I shared about this recurring nighttime tragedy, he paused and asked matter-of-factly, "Why don't you just move the chair?" It had never occurred to me, but that night, I took his advice, and—unsurprisingly—I never ran into it again.

Scripture offers similar counsel. In the fifth chapter of Proverbs, the hearer is counseled to avoid sin—the "chair"—by keeping his way *far* from the forbidden woman and *not even going near* the door of her house (Proverbs 5:8). For us moms who want to avoid sinning against our littlest neighbors, what might it look like to move the proverbial chair?

First, we need to take a look at our habits. When I have too much screen time, the overstimulation causes my fuse to get much shorter. When I don't get enough sleep, I am weepy and fatalistic. Now that I know these things about myself, I adjust accordingly to avoid the temptation to be unkind to my kids or to be withdrawn and unavailable to my family. In an election cycle, when I'm prone to more anxiety, I delete social media. I also maintain an early bedtime and commit to not binge-watch shows. It is wise to avoid things that interfere with the presence of mind necessary to respond as a Spirit-led person instead of reacting out of your sinful nature. Consider what these "chairs" may be for you—sugar intake, alcohol consumption, caffeine, overcommitment—and think about using that information to set boundaries or make adjustments that help you maintain agency. These things may also be circumstantial. Reevaluate the times that you struggle. What can you change?

- If you get hangry, maybe you need to carry protein-rich snacks with you.
- If you are easily overstimulated, you could get a pair of noise-reduction headphones or take time to go outside.
- If you lose your temper every morning with your kids, consider adjusting your routine. Do you need to allow more time? Make checklists to keep the kids on track?

Considering the connection between your unmet needs and your sinful behavior can help you avoid that situation so that you can live within your limits for the glory of God and the love of your littlest neighbor.

When I had three kids under six, I struggled with self-control during meal prep. It was too much for my brain to try to read and follow a recipe when I was constantly being interrupted at a time of day when my mind was tired and my kids were fussy (have you heard of the witching hour?). I "moved the chair" by creating a simple list of meals that I could cook without looking at a recipe. It took all the guesswork out of meal planning so that I could use my brain space for my kids. The list simplified a process in a season when I couldn't handle complex things. I recently smiled when I realized I was able to deviate from the plan and follow a more complicated recipe because my kids are now older and my mental health is much improved (thanks be to God). Our limits narrow and expand with our seasons. But wisdom allows us to recognize a change in capacity and respond accordingly.

Moving the Chair of Overwhelm

When I sense those changes in capacity, whether it's because of the start of summer or a new set of responsibilities for me or my husband, I have found that utilizing a daily habit tracker is extremely helpful for me in avoiding mental overload. I first started using it around the time of the solo bedtime story at the start of this chapter. The document was divided into three sections: morning, midday, and evening. It served as a sort of standard operating procedure, listing the things I needed to do within those windows. It eliminated the extra energy required to determine what needed to be done next, the time I lost picking up my phone when I felt lost, as well as the stress of to-dos piling up. For example, in the morning I was to start a load of laundry, at midday I moved that load to the dryer, and in the evening the tracker prompted me to fold and put away that load. This kept my laundry from piling up and created more mental margin for other things.

This tracker also gave me a clear picture of what I was able to accomplish in a day. The little check marks (or the lack of them) revealed how well I was doing the things that were most important so that I knew whether to add more tasks or commitments.

Ask yourself, "What responsibilities has God given *me*?" or "What can only *I* do?" Start with *only* those things and determine what day and what time of day they need to be done.

I send an editable version of this tracker to my newsletter subscribers to welcome them to the community, and I have heard from countless women that this document brought about significant change for them. They felt less overwhelmed and more able to be both present with their kids and in control of their reactions.

When You Can't Move the Chair

Maybe you are cynically wondering, "What if the metaphorical chair in the hallway is bolted to the floor?" What if it seems that you can't avoid the cause of the weakness that sin seems to prey on? What if your current circumstances feel overwhelming, and you can't avoid the situation that makes it seem nearly impossible to be the mom you're called to be? This chapter advises against pushing past your limits, but sometimes simply being a faithful mom pushes you past them. There were times when Jesus had to set aside his own bodily needs to fulfill a specific spiritual calling, such as when he fasted in the desert for forty days or stayed awake all night in prayer. There are certainly seasons when this is a requirement for a mom. It would be unfaithful to prioritize getting eight hours of sleep when we were supposed to be feeding a new baby every two to three hours or when one of our kids wakes up in the night with croup. In those times, as natural beings, we must scale back all that is not necessary in order to fulfill what is. But when our very calling requires us, for a time, to push past our limits for the sake of obedience and love of neighbor, we also must not allow the weakness of our natural bodies to cause us to forget the supernatural help that God provides. Rather than throwing up your hands because you feel like you can't get what you feel like you need to be faithful, let your weakness motivate you to be more on guard against sin and operate with a greater sense of dependence on God.

God Gave Your Kids a Human Mom

If you have ever wondered if you were ruining your kids because you couldn't be two places at once, or you didn't know the answer or didn't have the solution, or you had to step away, hear this: Having a human being for a mom isn't going to ruin your child, but having a mom who is unable to acknowledge and embrace that humanity is sure to have a negative impact. Conversely, a mom who readily admits her weakness, acknowledges her failure, and embraces her limits provides a powerful example to her kids of how to exist and thrive as a human being with both internal and external limits. May the Lord grant you the wisdom to discern and the humility to embrace your personal limitations, whatever they may be.

Parenting Connection

The Westminster Confession states that the responsibility of a parent is to care for their child "soul and body."[7] One way we can care for our kids is by helping them to live within their limits. If your four-year-old needs thirteen hours of sleep, but your lifestyle allows him to get only eleven each night, of course he will struggle to listen to instructions and regulate his emotions. The same is true of the effects of screen time on his brain or sugar on his nervous system. I know my kids need to move their bodies before we do an activity that requires them to be still for a while. One of the ways I love them as my littlest neighbors is to help their bodies get what they need according to the way God designed them.

Not only should we be aware of the bodily and developmental needs of our children, but we should also teach our *kids* to know and live within their limits. Recently, my husband took my kids to a golf tournament. After our four-year-old threw a fit, he told my husband, "I'm sorry, Daddy! I need protein!" We laughed about it, but I was glad my son was able to recognize his own hanger and verbalize what his body needed.

I applaud my kids as wise when they recognize their bodily cues for rest or food and respond by taking a nap or getting a snack. We talk frequently about the need for moderation when we consume sugar or caffeine because of the effect those things have on our ability to be sober-minded.

Try asking prompting questions and giving your kids the chance to check in with themselves and make their own decisions. When they want to have another piece of candy or read one more chapter before going to sleep, ask, "How do you think this will affect your ability to be in control of your actions?" When they fight bedtime, cite God's design for us, reminding them that a good night's sleep sets us up to have the best possible next day. Modeling living within your limits is also a powerful way to train your kids to live within their own limits for the glory of God. When I am beyond my limits because of a lack of sleep or any other factor, I tell my kids that I'm operating in weakness and let them know we're going to take it easy that day or that I may have to step away to take a deep breath before interacting with them.

Believe It for Your Motherhood

The gospel frees you from the need to prove yourself through what you can handle or accomplish. Paying attention to your limits and needs instead of pushing past them not only brings God glory as your designer but also enables you to fight temptation and live according to his commands by helping you maintain agency, or the ability to be sober-minded and self-controlled as you interact with your kids.

He said to me, "My grace is sufficient for you, for my power is made perfect in weakness." Therefore I will boast all the more gladly about my weaknesses, so that Christ's power may rest on me.

—2 Corinthians 12:9

Apply It to Your Parenting

- List the names of your children and their particular limits and needs.
- Introduce them to the word *agency*. Help them to pay attention to what affects their ability to feel in control of their actions and to act consistently with who they want to be (do the "walk it back" exercise with them).
- Present bedtimes and dietary limits as a kind invitation to flourishing and peace.
- Remember your child's physical needs as you address their behaviors. Try to ensure they have full bellies and get the sleep they need.

Chapter 3

Looking Beneath the Surface

I'm doing everything I know to do." Tears trickled down my cheeks as I confessed to my doctor, who also happened to be an elder in our church, that I just couldn't seem to get out from under the overwhelming weight I felt pressing down on me. I couldn't remember the last time I'd had a "good" day.

Amid my own postpartum mental health struggles, I read a story of a mother who had, a short time after giving birth, tragically killed her children and then taken her own life while her husband ran to get takeout. Friends and family all reported that this mother was loving, patient, and affectionate. This afflicted mother had a psychotic break and behaved entirely out of character.

After hearing this story, I was initially consumed with the question of responsibility. My biblical worldview told me that our actions reveal what is within our hearts. But this woman was obviously sick and not herself. I wondered, "Is postpartum rage something I need to repent of? Is it something I'm responsible for? Am I accountable for my behavior when under the influence of what seems like a disorder?" As mysterious as the answers to those questions felt, there was no question that my kids were being affected by my behavior.

During this period, I wrestled with shame. "If I trusted God more," I thought, "then I wouldn't be struggling like this." "If I was a more mature believer," I reasoned, "then I wouldn't be thinking the thoughts I'm thinking, or crying the way I am, or physically shaking with anxiety the way I am." To this point, I had failed to consider all that was happening within my body, and in doing so, I denied myself help.

I can't help but wonder how much harm to my children could have been avoided if I had understood sooner that my body and brain were so ravaged that I was not in my right mind. When presented with OB intake forms, I wasn't fully honest because I didn't want them to write any mental health diagnoses in my chart. I didn't want the label. I didn't want to be "crazy." Ironically, the fear of being crazy put me in a position of acting like and feeling like, well, a crazy person. But the story of this woman who took her own life and those of her children, apart from scaring me, gave me the courage to consider that something else might be going on beneath the surface.

Considering the Effects of the Fall on Our Bodies

Sometimes we may find that even though we're sampling all the items on the Healthy Mind Platter, we still struggle to remain in control. Or that even though we've cut back significantly on our commitments and simplified our lives as much as possible, everything still feels overwhelming. Or that even though we've used the daily habit tracker, we just can't seem to stay on task or avoid crumbling under the weight of to-dos.

The fall affects everything, remember? Just as the fall made indwelling sin a reality for all people, it also made sickness and suffering a reality for all people. We experience this reality in the common cold, stomach viruses, diminished neurological function, diseases, arthritis, hormonal imbalances, chronic pain, and mental illness. These aren't the good limits God made us with; they're tragic results of living in fallen bodies.

When pursuing change, we cannot fall into the ditch of addressing only the heart and mind or focusing solely on the physical body. We must address *both* our sinful flesh and our broken bodies simultaneously. Sanctification is something we pursue holistically.[1]

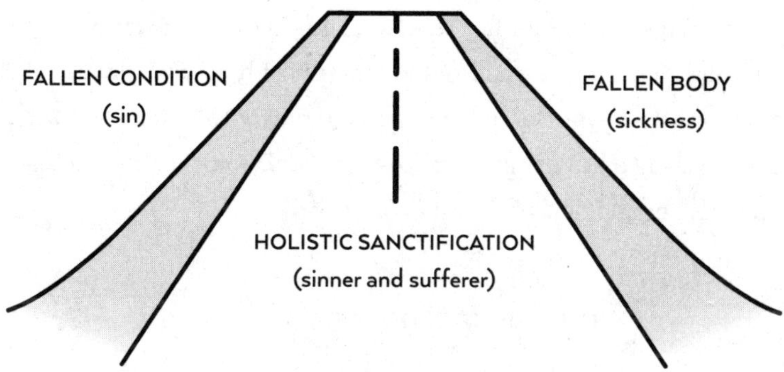

When it comes to issues like anxiety, depression, or even attention and irritability, differentiating between sin and sickness can feel tricky, but both of these realities of human existence must play into the way we think and live, even if we aren't able to discern where one begins and the other ends (which is often the case).[2]

Sinful behavior is a symptom of our fallen condition, *and* certain patterns of behavior can also be an indicator that something in our fallen *bodies* needs to be treated. For example, hormonal imbalances can affect mental health and therefore limit agency: hypothyroidism (too little thyroid hormone) is linked to low mood or depression, and hyperthyroidism (too much thyroid hormone) is usually linked to irritability and anxiety.

A few years ago, a friend of mine experienced a sudden onset of anxiety. She saw a doctor who discovered that she needed to be treated for a thyroid condition. When she started thyroid medication, her anxiety significantly diminished, allowing her to think more clearly and care for her kids with kindness and proactivity. Moments like these—when medical treatment restores balance, improving mental or behavioral health—are opportunities to praise God. They reveal and restore some of the order that he established in Eden.

Can insulin, hormone therapies, and thyroid medication make us holy? No. Can they aid in our pursuit of holiness? Absolutely. Seeking treatment can help women operate with a sounder mind, empowering them to make choices consistent with their worldview and walk in obedience to God's commands.

Pursuing Holiness and Healing

If my friend had looked at her short temper and paranoia as an isolated spiritual issue or a symptom of unbelief, she might have missed out on getting the help she needed. Sometimes this way of thinking suggests that if we simply had more faith or understood doctrine more, we wouldn't struggle like we are. When we think this way, we not only risk missing out on the comfort of God's mercy and compassionate care, but also might withhold from ourselves his particular grace of seeking relief or receiving the help we need for a bodily ailment.

Knowing a list of symptoms, even if they present as sinful behavior, can help us get the treatment or therapy we need to be more sober-minded and, therefore, more able to live consistently with God's commands. By saying this, I do not intend to negate the role of the Holy Spirit in empowering us to live holy lives; rather, I am pointing out that a healthy mind is more capable of choosing to respond in a Spirit-led way, rather than reacting out of sinful desires.

Conversely, if you find yourself thinking, "If I can just find a diagnosis, then I won't struggle like this," you risk missing out on the freedom of God's personal grace. Even with balanced hormones and an integrated mind, an optimally functioning body still needs the grace of God because it houses within it a soul plagued with a sinful condition. Being healed physically is not the same thing as being holy, and becoming more holy doesn't mean your physical or psychological challenges will disappear either. As we think about becoming the most godly moms we can be, who engage with our kids in a God-glorifying way, our pursuit of healing must not take the place of our pursuit of holiness; neither should our pursuit of holiness cause us to neglect our need for bodily healing. Because we're embodied souls, our body and spirit are connected in a way that necessitates considering each in addition to, not instead of, the other.

Which Is to Blame? Me or My Brain?

The book of Proverbs often alludes to the intertwining of a person's body with their emotional or spiritual state (see Proverbs 4:23; 14:30; 17:22). Our bodies influence the state of our hearts, and our hearts, in turn, influence the health of our bodies. And so, when we consider pursuing righteous living, it makes sense to think holistically rather than compartmentally. When we do, we can pursue holiness by responding to biblical conviction with confession while still seeking treatment for symptoms.

Sometimes we want to be able to tease this out, to take them one at a time, but the distinction between sinfulness and sickness is less like a thin line and more like an intertwined thread, like the Play-Doh colors my kids mix together that we have little hope of separating.

Still, we cannot underplay the role of our bodies and brains. A friend of mine who works with Alzheimer patients explained to me recently that, rather than revealing a person's true character, the behavioral expression of the disease, such as agitation or aggression, has far more to do with the part of the brain that is deteriorating. If the disease attacks the frontal lobe, she says, it doesn't matter how kind, sweet, or nurturing a person is—they will lash out because of their broken brain.

The gospel gives us the freedom to fill out psych eval forms with honesty to get the help we need. It also gives us the framework to confess and experience the joy that comes from repenting of what we feel guilty over to find absolution. We need God's mercy for our sickness and suffering, and we need his grace for our sinful thoughts and actions, but we don't necessarily need to understand where one begins and the other ends to receive that mercy and grace.

Surrendering to this mystery during my postpartum struggles with weepiness, overwhelm, and outbursts, I reached out to a therapist. My brain felt like it was broken, and I knew I needed help to rewire it. The psychotherapist I contacted described my brain as being overheated. She helped me pull over, so to speak, by reevaluating my capacity, which led to creating margin in my life and reducing my responsibilities so my brain wouldn't combust and burst into flames, burning my whole life down. If my brain was an overheated malfunctioning engine, the work she did with me was like a jug of water cooling, soothing, protecting, and restoring it.

It was helpful to think of my brain like this. Every time I've had a baby, I experienced intrusive suicidal thoughts and ideations. Each time I prepared to deliver, I hoped I had matured, become more disciplined, or become healthy enough that it wouldn't happen. But it always did. Understanding this from a perspective of bodily weakness because of the fall—namely, that my imbalanced hormones and sleep-deprived brain made it difficult to think rationally—helped me to recognize that I had more choices than my fatalistic, intrusive thoughts led me to believe. It provided me with the skill of separating my thoughts from my spiritual identity. I would say things like, "Ohp, there goes my brain again. This is just a blip. This is not who I am. This is just my brain doing what it does after I have a baby." Rather than wondering what those intrusive thoughts meant about *me spiritually*, I began to understand what they meant about *my body physically*.[3]

Some forms of sickness or suffering we can test and clearly diagnose, like hormonal imbalances, thyroid issues, genetic disorders, sleep apnea, or diabetes. Mental health stuff is harder to diagnose because there's often no clear and conclusive concrete test or scan. For psychiatric disorders, symptoms are simply grouped for the sake of understanding them or determining the best course of treatment. Sometimes mood or mental health disorders can be treated through counseling or specific therapies. Other times, as in my case, they might need more. Sometimes supplements or medication can be helpful.

Can a Pill Just Fix It?

Every person's situation is unique, so talk to your doctor before trying anything new. But knowing when medication or supplements or hormonal treatments might help isn't always black and white, even after input from a medical professional. Sometimes righteousness may be better pursued off medication so that we can truly feel our need and learn to depend more fully on God. Sometimes, however, righteousness is better pursued *on* medication so we can be of sound mind and, therefore, act in a Spirit-led way. It can help us be regulated enough to pray or read God's Word without a sense of impending doom or panic. Yet sometimes the side effects of medication become the grounds for an entirely different sin struggle (antidepressants can lead to agitation and hypervigilance, creating an occasion for rash speech and reactivity). Knowing whether to medicate isn't cut-and-dried. It requires wisdom, prayer, and wise counsel. After a year of therapy, that's the position I found myself in. I saw progress, sure, but my intrusive thoughts were mostly existential, so it was hard to find solace in the spiritual disciplines I once found so comforting.

That's how I ended up in that doctor's office. Even after a year of therapy, I was still easily overwhelmed. I was still weepy and distracted. I was still afraid of hurting my kids or myself. While I was much more aware of my choices in any given moment and felt a lot more in control of my actions, I was tired of fighting this constant internal battle and feared the long-term effects that this season of suffering and temporary weakness would have on me and my family.

I confessed to a friend of mine that taking medicine felt like faithlessness to me, like a cop-out. "Sometimes," she encouraged me, "when we have been treading water for so long, we get so worn out that all we can think about is drowning. But the goal is to get to land." She continued, "Medication is not a life preserver, but it gives you enough support to take a break from treading so hard so that you can catch your breath and think about which direction to kick. Sometimes," she said, "you have to regulate [*or calm*] the brain to retrain it." She asked me why, if I felt like I was drowning, and there was a pool noodle right next to me, I would be too prideful to grab on and kick to shore. "Medication is sometimes the form that God's mercy takes for his suffering children." She said gently, "It isn't going to do all the work, but it can help you get to a point where *you* can do the work."

It's impossible to fully know how psychological or physical factors play into the way you conduct yourself as you strive to be a Christlike mom. Only God knows when a psychological issue stretches past context and motive to describe the *cause* of sinful behavior.[4] But the fact that it's a mystery doesn't mean there isn't some benefit to considering that a bodily issue might be making the fight against sin more difficult and that some relief might be experienced by seeking healing for that bodily ailment. For a long time, feeling like I needed to have this fully fleshed out kept me from getting the help I needed.

The two greatest commandments are to love God and love neighbor. Sometimes obedience to those commandments means pursuing care for the body that carries them out. How can you do this?

- Schedule a checkup.
- Fill out the psych form at your doctor's office honestly.
- Check your hormone levels.
- See if you may have vitamin deficiencies that affect mood or sleep.
- Make an appointment with a mental health professional to screen for disorders treatable with therapy or medication.
- You may even need a brain scan to check for deterioration or a tumor.

The Christian life necessitates a pursuit of holiness. In that pursuit, you should still practice repentance and seek to turn from your sin. But to neglect to care for the body that carries out biblical commands is an act of faithlessness. Conversely, we might be so focused on the healing of our bodies that we neglect the care of our souls. Propelled by the desire to eliminate sinful behaviors, we might hunt hard for diagnoses or obsess over our diet to the point that we look at those things as our functional saviors. I sincerely hope that taking one of these actions brings you relief. Yet even if treatment helps to restore equilibrium, remember, a label isn't absolution; it is an aid in your pursuit of holiness. So as you employ the tools of diet, exercise, and medical care, don't neglect the command to abide in Christ, to repent and believe.

What If You Can't Relieve Your Symptoms?

Understanding the fall offers a framework to face the sickness and suffering that we can't treat or do anything about. We've talked a lot in this chapter about how sickness might hinder sanctification, but it can also aid in our sanctification. We'll explore this more in a later chapter, but suffering is one of God's chosen instruments for making us more like Jesus. In a letter to the Corinthians, the apostle Paul talks about a "thorn" in his flesh. It's not clear whether this was a temptation to sin or a struggle with suffering, but what is clear is that he asked God to take it away, but his petition wasn't granted (2 Corinthians 12:7–10).

Like Paul, maybe you have pleaded with God to provide relief from certain ailments, but they remain. Some things you cannot control and cannot fix. Not everything can be healed or even treated on this side of heaven. But because God's grace is sufficient and his power is made perfect in weakness, we can say with Paul, "I will boast all the more gladly about my weaknesses, so that Christ's power may rest on me. . . . For when I am weak, then I am strong" (2 Corinthians 12:9–10).

Perhaps you fear the effect that your particular ailment or weakness will have on your kids. My friend Samantha has cancer, and it's incurable. She worries about the effect that years of watching her suffer and ultimately die will have on her three young children. My friend Martha has chronic pain. She cannot participate in field day events or attend her kids' traveling sporting events. But both women have a powerful perspective. These two women look at their suffering not just as an effect of the fall but as an opportunity to give glory to God. These moms are present and attentive to their kids; they teach their children the gospel, and they model what it looks like to lament the effects of the fall and still live a full and abundant life, even if the cards they've been dealt aren't what they would've chosen.

My son came to me recently with an outlandish existential question—one that I've had too. And in that moment, I teared up, feeling a deep connection to him. I didn't know anyone else in the world thought that way. Though I didn't share that with him, I later confided in a friend that I felt responsible, like I'd somehow passed on my plague of existential anxiety, and that I felt sorry for him. "Oh, I'm so relieved for him," she commented, tenderness displayed in the creases beside her eyes, "that he has a mom who will receive his questions with tenderness and have the courage to explore them together. Who is more equipped than you? He has a mom who will empathize and never dismiss him or make him feel crazy."[5]

Even if you despise your weakness, being robbed of your feeling of strength and wisdom can actually be a gift to your parenting. The irony is that the very thing we fear is ruining our kids is potentially one of our greatest gifts to them because it leads us to parent from a place of weakness, humility, and dependence on God. As you hold in tension the realities of fallenness and sinfulness, you can be honest with your kids and teach them to observe these realities in their own lives and hearts. And you can trust that God will use any sickness and suffering to shape your children into who he made them to be.

Parenting Connection

When one of my sons was about six years old, a set of symptoms led to the discovery of a sensory processing disorder. When I talked to our pediatrician about some of these behavior patterns, he recommended occupational therapy. Our son's therapist approached his struggle holistically, offering tools to help him manage his behavior in the moment, allowing him to act in the godly way he wanted to, while also teaching him how to take responsibility for his actions.

The gospel framework we have as believers also helped us deal with the intense feelings of shame that followed his outbursts. My son needed treatment for his brain and nervous system and absolution for (not dismissal of) the actions he carried out while out of control. He experienced the kindness of God in the form of both grace for his sin and mercy for his misery. My husband and I were committed to making sure he had access to both.

Our kids, just like us, simultaneously need moral guidance (because they are born with a sinful condition) and compassionate physical care (because they are born into bodies affected by the fall).

If your child has a sudden change in behavior, think about what their body is going through. Weepiness or delusional behavior often alerts me that my kids have an ear infection or a fever. On occasion, their behaviors have alerted me to a nutrient deficiency. These don't excuse negative behavior, but they provide explanations for it and point to ways to care for our kids. Two things are true at once. You can dignify your kids by treating them as embodied human beings. Our children are full humans who are *simultaneously* sufferers who need support and fallen sinners who need shepherding. You can be their compassionate guide and caregiver. Give them the gospel and give them the bodily care they need too.

Believe It for Your Motherhood

God is filled with compassion for you and the ways you have been impacted by the fall. As you seek to become a more Christlike mom, you can pursue sanctification holistically by seeking care for your body and brain with which you love God and your littlest neighbors.

My flesh and my heart may fail,
but God is the strength of my heart
and my portion forever.
—Psalm 73:26

Apply It to Your Parenting

- List the names of your children and their particular challenges and ailments.

- Routinely discuss your kids' concerning behavior with their pediatrician.
- When a child acts out of character, before reacting harshly, consider what might be going on below the surface (check their temperature, etc.). They may need care before correction.
- Whenever possible, empathize with your child even as you correct them.

Chapter 4

Engaging Your Story

Ten years ago, my sister Jamison noticed that her infant son seemed to be panting. A short while later, he was airlifted to a hospital. She was not allowed to ride in the helicopter with him, so she drove an hour and a half in terror, not knowing if her baby would even be alive when she got to the hospital. He needed emergency open-heart surgery. Over the next few weeks, she felt powerless as she watched him suffer his difficult-to-manage pain.

As Jamison learned how to strategically pick up, breastfeed, and administer meds to this baby with a zipper-like wound on his chest, she was also caring for his active two-year-old brother, who was letting her know—in all the ways that two-year-olds do—how much he had missed her during her hospital stay. Two weeks into this hard transition, my nephew's physical symptoms revealed that the surgical repair to his mitral valve had not held. They headed back to the hospital for another open-heart operation. This one held, but they knew he'd need another in a handful of years.

A while ago, I listened as she vented about her kids' behavior and lamented her own reactions.

"When's the next cardiology appointment?" I asked when she finished.

"A week," she answered.

"Well, there you have it," I responded matter-of-factly.

Each time my nephew has a heart appointment, my sister struggles to be patient with her children. "It took a long time to realize that my anxiety was manifesting itself as anger," she told me recently. "When he had an appointment coming up, even the sound of my kids laughing would send me over the edge. It made me feel out of control, and I so desperately needed to feel like I was in control—since I had so little control over the health of my son."

Jamison also noticed that in situations where her kids are in perceived danger, like when they are mountain biking or even when another operation is approaching, she found herself not in fight mode but in a sort of floating mode. She described feeling cut off and emotionally distant from her kids in an almost self-protective way. She was tempted to zone out, becoming absorbed in novels, shows, or other methods of escape.

My sister confessed her fits of rage repeatedly. She also lamented and regretted her lack of emotional availability and loving presence with her kids during moments that were supposed to be "fun." But what she failed to do for a long time was to recognize that her anger and ambivalence were both secondary emotions. If either of those aspects of her motherhood were going to change, she needed Jesus to minister to the fearful and wounded part of her that anger and ambivalence were trying to protect.

Sometimes, in our worst moments of motherhood, we identify so strongly as the villain that we fail to recognize we are also victims. Listen to me again, friend: It is true that you are a sinner whose ungodly actions negatively affect your kids, *and* you are simultaneously a sufferer—not just because of the effects of the fall on your body but also because your heart, mind, and nervous system have been affected by the sins of others and by the harsh, hard realities of living in a fallen world. To become the best mom you can possibly be for your kids, you don't just need correction for the wrong you do, you also need care for the wrong you've experienced.[1] Pausing to consider your pain isn't a cop-out or even an aside as we talk about you becoming the mom you want to be. Ministering to our woundedness is another way God changes us. Engaging your story is an essential part of being a mom who is able to show up to the task of parenting with intentionality instead of reactivity.

Wounds and Gaps

Perhaps upon reading my sister's story, you were immediately able to identify your own experiences of trauma and pain. But maybe you suspect that this chapter might not be relevant to you because, comparatively, you feel as if you've had a relatively trouble-free life. Just because you haven't experienced a big-*T* trauma, don't be so quick to dismiss your own experiences as insignificant, and don't underestimate the seemingly irrelevant pieces of your story. Get curious about the way your own past experiences in a fallen world affect how you interact with it today.

In a perfect world, one untainted by sin, there would be no wounds or gaps in your history. But because you were raised by imperfect people in a fallen world, your story inevitably includes them. By wounds, I mean the things that have happened to you that hurt you. By gaps, I mean the care that should have been given that was withheld from you.

Let's say that as a five-year-old you fell while riding your scooter and scraped your knee. You felt the chaos of pain and stood and ran (as best you could on that banged-up leg) to find a caregiver. If your caregiver was healthy and well-adjusted, then she likely scooped you up, shushed and comforted you, and maybe even encouraged you to take deep breaths while hugging and soothing you. Once you calmed down, as she applied antibiotic and a bandage, she might have asked you to tell her the story of what happened. After you recalled the whole event, maybe she told you that you were brave and that she was sorry that had happened. You received comfort, were able to process and organize the event in your brain, and hopped back on your scooter.

Even as I tell that imaginary story, you might sense the wounds and gaps in your own story because you know how that scenario would have gone in your home. Let's replay this event with a different outcome. Let's say you searched and searched, but no one was available to you. Maybe your caregiver was at work or passed out on the couch. Because you didn't have the skills to self-regulate and a stable, supportive person with whom to coregulate, this event was stored unprocessed and unorganized in your brain. As a result, you didn't want to ride your scooter anymore. This experience could be categorized as a **gap** in your care as a child.

Now, let's say you limped through your front door, spotted your mom, and cried out, "Mom, I fell off my scooter!" But instead of opening her arms to you, she shamed you. "Haven't I told you to be careful? Do you have to scream about everything? The only reason you should be crying like that is if you are missing a limb! You'll never make it in this world if you cry like a baby every time you get a little cut." This event could now be classified as a **wound**.

Your experiences of suffering and the way you interact with and react to the world around you are more closely connected than you may realize. Now, I'm not a neuroscientist. And I'm not a psychologist. But the science is simple enough for me to understand and be truly helped by it. And I hope I can communicate it clearly enough that it might serve you too.

Based on the relationships we have with our caregivers as children, we develop patterns and frameworks for relating to others (these are often referred to as "attachment styles" if you want to do more research). Our past experiences also create implicit memories that influence our behavior at a subconscious level. Neurological pathways carved during pain and hardship shape our future thought patterns and anxieties (the same way water follows the troughs and tunnels I dig in the sand when my boys and I make moats for our castles on the beach). Events that we're unable to process and regulate, even if they don't seem like they would be classified as "traumatic," are stored as trauma that embeds itself into our bodies so that our reactions to similar stimuli in the future can feel almost reflexive.

In my worst moments of motherhood, I have often felt like I didn't deserve to seek out or receive God's love and care, but the moments when we feel most unworthy of his love are arguably the moments we most need to receive it. If you want to experience true and lasting change from the inside out, it's important to deal with the wounds or gaps that may lurk beneath your problematic behaviors. These could be events in your past, like bullying, abuse, or parental relationships, or they may be current experiences, like a lack of support, or wounding words, or any of the general hardships we talked about in the last chapter. Just as certain sin patterns can alert us to the need to tend to sickness within our bodies, they can also be coping mechanisms that signal our need to receive care for the impact of our wounds and gaps.

How might the impact of these hard realities show up?

- feeling emotionally distant from or unavailable to help your kids because you're consumed with your internal experience
- experiencing disproportionate rage when your child is defiant or lashes out at you
- isolating yourself from others for fear of rejection
- feeling helpless or inadequate as a parent because your parent infantilized you
- processing your child's normal hardship, like tears at separation, as trauma because of your own past experiences
- struggling to set or hold loving boundaries with your kids because your own boundaries were violated
- sabotaging moments that feel happy or healthy because chaos feels more familiar

If you're like me, when these feelings and behaviors show up, you start—as a mentor of mine likes to say—"Shoulding" all over yourself.

- *I should be more available to my kids.*
- *I should be more patient.*
- *I should try harder to do playdates and be involved at their school.*
- *I should be able to leave my kid without feeling like I'm traumatizing them.*
- *I should be more consistent.*
- *I should be able to just enjoy moments like this. I always ruin them!*

"Shoulding" on yourself is a symptom of shame. And shame, as we've discussed, keeps us from changing. "Shoulding" leads to condemnation rather than curiosity, which keeps us from processing this kind of information as clues leading us to receive the help we need to heal and grow. Our coping mechanisms, or the behaviors associated with the pain beneath them, are not the only part of us that needs to change. The wounded parts also need to be healed. Our sinning parts are often closely connected with our suffering parts.[2] We want to be safe from wounds, and we want to be comforted in gaps, but the problem is that we try to meet our own needs instead of depending on our Father. If we treat our safety and comfort as ultimate, we will sin to get them. If we see *God* as ultimate, we will receive safety and comfort from him and live righteously out of that secure attachment and felt safety.

Showing Up with Creativity, Care, and Concern for Our Kids

In her memoir *The Hiding Place,* World War II survivor Corrie ten Boom recounts a conversation she had with her father when she was a preteen. She asked a question about something that her father thought Corrie was too young to understand. She recalls the interaction like this:

> He turned to look at me, as he always did when answering a question, but to my surprise, he said nothing. At last he stood up, lifted his traveling case off the floor, and set it on the floor.
>
> "Will you carry it off the train, Corrie?" he said.
>
> I stood up and tugged at it. It was crammed with the watches and spare parts he had purchased that morning.

> "It's too heavy," I said.
>
> "Yes," he said, "and it would be a pretty poor father who would ask his little girl to carry such a load. It's the same way, Corrie, with knowledge. Some knowledge is too heavy for children. When you are older and stronger, you can bear it. For now, you must trust me to carry it for you."[3]

When one of my sons was seven, I took him to Washington, DC, to see his favorite artist in concert with the National Symphony Orchestra. This scene between Corrie and her dad popped into my mind as I found myself short-tempered and dismissive of his many questions, preoccupied with navigating Ubers and alleyways and riddled with anxiety. Corrie's father, in contrast, had been present, attentive, and deliberate. His concern was for his daughter. Rather than being absorbed in his inner world, this father was available and able to focus his complete attention on Corrie, responding to her question with creativity and care.

Motherhood often comes with more present trouble than navigating a strange city with a curious child in tow. How can we parent with presence and creativity while navigating the grief of miscarriage or the stress of a difficult marriage? How can we love our kids well under the weight of their unique medical or behavioral demands? How can we respond with care while navigating betrayal or the death of a loved one?

My friend Anna describes the struggle well:

> I was thirty-four when, together, my parents told me my dad had an ongoing affair when I was eight. Married ten years myself at the time, with three young kids at home, my world was rocked. For months, I would randomly remember and feel grief and sadness.

> I felt like I couldn't function with my kids. I was quicker to anger and more protective. I wanted to cry, but instead, I yelled. My grief needed time—time I felt like I didn't have with motherhood, work, and general life.

Learning of her father's affair narrowed Anna's capacity for intentional living. The term "window of tolerance," developed by psychologist Dan Siegel, refers to the zone in which people are most able to thrive, being flexible, present, and emotionally regulated, like Corrie's father.[4] When a person is within their window of tolerance, they have access to their executive function skills and can problem-solve, be creative, regulate their emotions, organize, and plan.

As we learn to view motherhood as an embodied experience, in addition to acknowledging our limitations, sinful desires, and ailments, we should also consider how our past and even present experiences impact our nervous systems and, therefore, inform our behavior.

When we experience stress in the present or when something triggers a subconscious memory of something painful, scary, chaotic, or confusing, we may find ourselves acting rashly or becoming distant or numb, even in situations where we previously did not struggle to problem-solve or stay present and remain calm.

That's what happened to Anna when she learned of her dad's affair. Her world was rocked because a source of security, safety, and rest—the character of her father—was suddenly called into question. The foundation of her "loving family" felt shaken. Suddenly, nothing felt trustworthy or safe. And so she shifted out of her window of tolerance.

This is what happens to my sister when she perceives that her kids are in danger. And that's what happens when *you* experience any sort of external stress that touches on the raw spot of a wound or gap in your past.

Maybe this all seems obvious to you, even if you were unfamiliar with the phrase "window of tolerance" until a few moments ago. *Of course external stress can narrow our capacity to respond to our kids the way we want to.* But knowing this conceptually is not enough. We have to know what to *do* with that information in order to regain our agency and respond in a way that is motivated by a love of God and neighbor instead of instinctive self-preservation and self-protection.

To learn how to recognize and deal with the effects of a fallen world on your nervous system and regain your agency, let's consider the experience of my friend Margaret. Your story and experience might be different from Margaret's, but you can use the same tools that she has employed to show up as a healthy, present, loving, creative mom for your kids.

A Case Study: Margaret

Margaret is the mom of three children under ten. A few months ago, Margaret noticed that when her kids get really silly in the car, she becomes extremely anxious. She tried to suppress and dismiss this feeling, but every time she felt it, the same thing happened: The longer they laughed, the more upset she felt, until finally she exploded, screaming something along the lines of "Shut up!"

Tool #1: Awareness

Being aware of your own window of tolerance helps you recognize when you're outside of it and, therefore, use effective tools to expand it. So what does it feel like to be outside of that window? How can you tell when this is happening?

On either side of this window are states of **hypoarousal**, an emotional state characterized by withdrawal, indifference, depression, numbness, or shame, and **hyperarousal**, an emotional state characterized by agitation, distress, overwhelm, anger, anxiety, or hypervigilance. In hypoarousal, we give up and disengage because we feel powerless. In hyperarousal, we try to control or fight off the perceived threat.[5] (We just saw this, remember? But now we have definitions: Hypoarousal = my sister numbing out when her kids are in perceived danger. Hyperarousal = my sister becoming angry and reactive approaching a hospital or doctor's appointment).

My in-laws keep a key in a lockbox on their porch so we can come and go as we please. When I use the key to open the door, I am occasionally surprised to hear the alarm start beeping (they don't always use the security system). Each time this happens, I am affected. I was present when they were robbed one evening years ago. My body hears the alarm and my internal alarm goes off, preparing me for danger when there is in fact no real threat.

The alarm is going off not because an unwelcome intruder is present but simply because my kids and I walked into the house. If I walk around the corner to the keypad and punch in the code, an automated voice says, "Alarm off." Then we can grab some towels and enjoy playing in the pool in the backyard.

Being triggered by past experiences is like this. You may have heard the expression "Neurons that fire together wire together."[6] This means that our brains store memory in such a way that an experience with a certain stimulus can influence our reaction to a related stimulus later in life. This is why our friend Ryan, who did medevac missions during Operation Iraqi Freedom, jumps whenever a fly gets caught in the bug zapper at our house. The popping sound that we associate with successfully ridding our home of bugs is subconsciously processed by Ryan's brain as danger. This type of long-term memory is called implicit memory, and it influences our behavior subconsciously.

Your nervous system operates much like that security system. Taking necessary action during the beeping part can help you avoid the chaos of the full-blown alarm. So, what does this look like? It's paying attention to your body's responses and reactions to certain stimuli, even if you're not quite sure what the stimuli is. What exactly might you be looking for?

- a tight jaw
- a quickened heart rate
- itching sensations
- stomach pain or butterflies
- holding your breath
- heart palpitations
- a tingling sensation in your limbs
- a headache

Rather than ignoring these things, pay attention to them as you would the beeping of a security system so that you can accurately process whatever is triggering that alarm and then punch in the code, letting your body know you're safe.

When Margaret's kids got loud in the car, her body functioned like the alarm at my in-laws' house, alerting her to a threat that wasn't actually present because it was triggered by some past experience. Margaret learned to recognize the bodily warning signs leading up to the moment she would scream at her kids. She learned to pay attention to the sensations she experienced before she screamed. She felt hot. Her heart rate would increase. She sometimes heard pounding in her ears. Her skin felt tight. She felt the urge to clench her fists or dig her fingers into the steering wheel.

Once Margaret identified these signals, she was able to pay attention to what *emotions* those physiological symptoms represented. Margaret could then name the feeling, so she could tame the feeling[7]: "I feel out of control and afraid." Naming those emotions helped Margaret deal with her fear and overwhelm instead of letting her fear and overwhelm drive her to deal with her kids in a way she didn't want to. Noticing these signals allowed Margaret to soothe herself or be soothed by the Holy Spirit. She could prayerfully punch in the code instead of blowing up in self-protection.

Bodily awareness is a big part of learning to stay within your window of tolerance.[8] So what does the experience of coming to the edge of *your* window of tolerance feel like? What does your body do when your internal alarm starts to sound? Practice paying attention to your body's signals, which alert you to a need for care. Once you can recognize these warning signs, or bodily cues for help, you can name the emotions and feelings to which they're alerting you and practice self-regulation tactics to stay within your window of tolerance and maintain self-control.

Tool #2: Self-Compassion and Regulation

Once we're aware of our body's warning signs, we can use self-compassion and regulation to get back into our window of tolerance. Now, to many of us, self-compassion feels like a kitschy, secular woo-woo phrase. But really, practicing self-compassion is about agreeing with God and responding to ourselves as he does. Think of self-compassion as a godly alternative to self-worship or self-loathing. After all, the command is "Love your neighbor *as* yourself," not "Love your neighbor, *not* yourself."[9]

When Margaret's internal alarm went off, rather than acting out of those emotions, she learned to receive God's care for them. Margaret would utter a prayer to a God she knew was listening, like an overwhelmed little kid who just fell off her scooter. "God, this moment feels really hard. I don't like feeling out of control. I feel trapped in this car right now."

Then Margaret would feel God's compassion for her, recalling Scripture about his heart toward her from notecards she now kept on her dashboard.

> As for me, I am poor and needy,
>   but the Lord takes thought for me.
> You are my help and my deliverer. (Psalm 40:17 ESV)

> You are my strength, my rock, my fortress, my deliverer, my refuge, my shield, my stronghold. I call upon the Lord and I am safe. (Psalm 18:2–4 paraphrased).

Margaret would take deep breaths and hear God speak from his Word:

> Be still, and know that I am God. (Psalm 46:10)

Then Margaret, rather than feeling helpless, would appeal to God for help, praying, "Help me to see my children as neighbors to love, not threats to subdue. Please give me your peace and help me to participate in their joy instead of feeling threatened by it."

In moments that feel chaotic, Margaret now experiences God's peace. His presence and his Word help her to regulate her emotions and calm her nervous system. Then she can respond intentionally rather than reacting instinctively.

When Margaret's kids got loud in the car, she went into a state of hyperarousal. When you experience agitation, distress, overwhelm, anger, anxiety, or hypervigilance, you, like Margaret, need methods to calm and soothe yourself. One effective method is to take deep breaths. Deep breathing sends a signal to your nervous system that you are safe. When you inhale, the contraction and relaxation of your diaphragm simulates your vagus nerve, which activates the relaxation response of your parasympathetic nervous system. This counters the fight-or-flight response of your sympathetic nervous system, thus bringing you back into your window of tolerance.[10]

> Help with Hyperarousal
>
> Take a deep breath.
> Practice four-corner breathing.
> Give yourself a gentle hug.
> Recite Scripture out loud.

The next time you find yourself in a state of hyperarousal, consider trying one or all of these practices:

1. Practice "box" or "four corner" breathing:

- Inhale for four seconds. →
- Hold your breath for four seconds. ↓
- Breathe out for four seconds. ←
- Hold your breath for four seconds. ↑

This practice is scientifically proven to calm your nervous system, helping you become more aware of other choices you can make as you respond to your kids than simply fighting or fleeing.

2. Use calming touch: It may feel silly, but you can give yourself a gentle hug or ask someone, even one of your kids, to hold your hand. A reassuring touch, even from yourself, can signal safety to your brain.
3. Recite Scripture out loud: Hearing God's words can help calm you, just like a father soothing his child. You can keep notecards taped in areas where you experience overwhelm or even on a keychain for quick reference.

Conversely, if you're in a state of hypoarousal, which happened to me recently after I realized I had missed an appointment, what you need is stimulation. This can mean running cold water over your hands, lightly tapping your shoulders, playing upbeat worship music, or moving your body. In my case, I stood up, turned on worship music, and danced until I no longer felt like I wanted to curl up in bed and cry. Regulation is like repentance: It's turning away from what we place our trust in—controlling our environment or comforting ourselves—and running back to God to rest in his control and care for us.

Help with Hypoarousal

Run cold water over your hands.
Lightly tap your shoulders.
Play upbeat worship music.
Move your body (jumping jacks or dancing).

God made your nervous system. He loves the scared, lonely little kid alive in your memory and longs for you to experience the comfort of his safety. In the hard moments, remember that God is filled with compassion for you as his child. He doesn't shame you for the way you're affected; he knows your wounds and gaps. Let your experience of those difficult, dysregulating moments be transformed by his compassion and care for you.

We slip outside the window of tolerance because we are afraid or feel vulnerable. We cope by either trying to manage our environment or our kids by neutralizing threats like the Terminator, or cutting ourselves off and withdrawing for the sake of self-protection. As moms, this often means creating wounds or gaps in the lives of our own children. The goal for you and me as followers of Jesus is to entrust ourselves to the God who is sovereign over all and who cares for us. We do this by naming our emotions and expressing them heavenward, feeling seen and felt by God as we experience his compassion and practice self-compassion. Then, once we're regulated, we can get curious.

Tool #3: Curiosity

Once Margaret shifted from condemning herself for her feelings to soothing her triggered nervous system, she started getting curious about why the stimuli of her noisy kids in the car affected her. According to Proverbs 20:5, "The purposes of a person's heart are deep waters, but one who has insight draws them out." We are wise when we, like the writer of Psalm 139, ask God to search our hearts and reveal their motivations to us (Psalm 139:23–24).

Once you return to your window of tolerance after a triggering moment, get curious about what stimuli set off the alarm within you. That process may sound like this:

- "Hmm, this really affected me.
- I wonder why.
- Might this be pointing to a wound or a gap in my story?

- I wonder what it is about this event that might be causing me to feel threatened?"

The answer *may* just be that you love being in control, being on time, or hearing your song on the radio. *But* ask the Lord to reveal whether anything in your past needs to be processed or healed for you to be able to relate to your children as little neighbors to love instead of threats to neutralize.

After Margaret thought for a while about why she reacted to the loud laughter of her kids in the car, one day a light bulb went off when Margaret's mom casually mentioned how her dad, Margaret's grandfather, would yell and threaten to spank his children for *speaking* in the car or touching the windows.

Margaret then made a connection to her own childhood. When Margaret and her siblings started laughing in the car, her mom often threatened to pull over and spank them if they didn't settle down and be quiet. This explained why, as an adult, Margaret would react as if she was in danger when her own kids got really silly in the car.

What would have happened if Margaret hadn't been curious? What if she shamed herself instead? What if Margaret, rather than learning to recognize the effects of her childhood, simply continued to beat herself up for being affected?

In his book on the effect of trauma on the brain, mind, and body, Dr. Bessel van der Kolk writes, "The more people try to push away and ignore internal warning signs, the more likely [those warning signs] are to take over and leave them bewildered, confused, and ashamed. People who cannot comfortably notice what is going on inside become vulnerable to respond to any sensory shift either by shutting down or by going into a panic—they develop a fear of fear itself."[11]

You might think your negative experiences weren't traumatic, but minimizing our pain or trying to make our experiences seem smaller doesn't reduce their effect on us. Rather, the opposite is true. The more we suppress our suffering and ignore the "why" behind our reactions, the less in control we are. When we understand what is happening and *why* it is happening, instead of *reacting*, controlled by our nervous system, we can *respond*, led by the Holy Spirit.

God knows all the particulars of your wounded and wandering heart. And he has compassion enough for both your sinful and your suffering parts. He has the wisdom to guide you through all the psychological and physiological stuff you can't see that's motivating your actions. As you seek to discern the intentions and motivations of your own heart, it may be helpful to make a timeline of your life, marking major events and considering what certain seasons (elementary school, adolescence, etc.) felt like.

Over time, as Margaret processed her feelings with the Lord, new pathways formed in her brain. Today, Margaret is learning to associate her children's laughter in the car with happiness and fun. Sometimes, thanks be to God, she even laughs with them.

The News and Your Nervous System

Not every strong reaction we experience arises from a wound or a gap in our story. But the events of a fallen world don't have to affect us personally to impact our motherhood. Watching a tragic news story or being aware of a great global injustice has an effect on our nervous system. But even if the corresponding emotional reaction we have to any given stimulus is fully logical in the present and proportionate to the provocation, we still need to be regulated and sober-minded as we interact with our kids.

The day after I heard of a tragedy a few states away that involved the loss of several young girls, my newsfeed was flooded with exhortations to "hold [my] babies close." I wondered what was wrong with me as I felt strangely withdrawn and emotionally distant and easily agitated by and short-tempered with my kids, while those grieving moms would give anything to be with their little girls. But that ping-ponging state of my nervous system was grief coming out sideways. Once I stopped "shoulding" all over myself and got curious, I realized I needed to make space to process and cry. My boys and I needed to take it easy on ourselves by going somewhere they wouldn't require a lot of correction or redirection so that I could have room to process even as I was with them. I also created some distance between myself and this event by not looking at my phone for a while (this was another way to acknowledge and embrace my capacity and humanity).

Recognizing how a fallen world affects us (bodily awareness)—even through news from across the country or halfway around the world—helps us to be aware of what is happening within us emotionally. Curiosity about that data enables us to recognize we are withdrawn because of sad news or angry because of injustice. This protects our kids from those emotions coming out sideways.

The Measurable Impact of Curiosity

The power of curiosity showed up in a meaningful way for me recently. Over the course of a few months of paying attention to when I was affected, I noticed a theme. I noticed that being important to people really mattered to me, and when someone else seemed more important to the people I was close to, I often felt anxious and insecure.

For example, whenever I heard my dearest friend refer to someone else as her "best" friend, I felt sort of panicked and would instinctively try harder or cling tighter. Because of wounds and gaps in my childhood and the events of my story, I used defined relationships to keep myself safe or to feel secure (for example, being someone's "girlfriend" or "best" friend or "favorite" person).

Since that discovery, I've been working on developing a more secure attachment style by rooting myself in God's love and care so that I can love people instead of using them. This story feels hard to share, but I want to show the value of engaging your story for the sake of your kids. Anger is easy to see, but these less obvious destructive ways of interacting with our kids, such as triangulation, gossip, or parentification, although subtler than anger, can still have a negative impact on them.[12]

Recently when I was putting my son to bed, he told me how much he loves his babysitter. He talked and talked about all the special things they had done together that day and how she does his bedtime routine. Then he asked me to do something in his bedtime routine the way she did it, instead of what I usually do. Envy bubbled up within me, and I immediately felt threatened. The words were on the tip of my tongue: "But you love Mommy *more*, right?"

Suddenly, I was bombarded with temptations masking themselves as strategies to keep myself emotionally and relationally safe. I was tempted to speak negatively about his sitter so that my position as his first, best, and preferred person would be protected. But **awareness** in that moment moved me to pause. I took a deep breath, reminded myself that I was beloved, and harnessed the power of **curiosity** and **compassion**. I wondered, "Why am I responding this way?" However, as a direct result of the personal exploration of the wounds and gaps in my own story, I recognized where this need for reassurance was coming from, and besides being sad, I could also name it as both sinful and inappropriate. I was seeking identity from my child instead of resting in my identity as a child of God. And that is not a burden my son needs to bear or a role he needs to take on.

Knowing my story and understanding why it is triggering to not be someone "special" or to feel like my place or role is being threatened enabled me to respond in a godly way instead of a sinful way.

I chose in that moment to see this boy as a child of God, not just possessively as *my* son. I focused on the fact that I am loved by God, special to my Father, and secure in the most important relationship I have. I received his compassion for the wounded little girl inside me, so desperate to be loved and chosen. And I rested in his assurance of pardon for running to the idol of the approval of others instead of resting in him. I took a deep breath. "I am so glad you have a babysitter you love. What a tremendous gift. Tell me again how she does it?"

That night, the trigger was his babysitter, but I'm hopeful that as my boys grow up and, Lord willing, get married, I will be a mother-in-law with a secure identity and with love for their wives instead of a spirit of competition and offense. Awareness of my emotions and curiosity about the impact of the pain of my past help me to act in a God-honoring way in the present and, hopefully, will help me do so in the future as well.

Tool #4: Processing

Once we become curious about what elicits an emotional reaction, rather than suppressing it, we can process that pain, fear, or confusion through prayer. The behavior you want to change could be a coping mechanism you've come to rely on to keep a wounded part of you safe. Even as you repent of the sin, ask it to step aside so that you can access the hurting part it's trying to protect. It might even be helpful to try to picture this part. Is it a hurting little girl? A neglected child? An abandoned young woman? Whoever you find, bring that hurting part of you to Jesus. Let that part of you tell Jesus all about what has been painful. In return, let him speak words of comfort and care to her from his Word. Maybe she needs to hear, "I will never leave you nor forsake you" (Hebrews 13:5 ESV), or "You are precious in my eyes, and honored, and I love you" (Isaiah 43:4 ESV). Or perhaps, "Fear not, for I am with you; don't be sad, for I'm your God. I'll give you the strength you need. I will help you. I'll hold you up. You're not alone" (Isaiah 41:10, paraphrased). You can speak these verses aloud, write them in a journal, or pray them in your heart.

Some aspects of life and motherhood are unimaginably hard, and the Bible is incredibly honest about these hardships on this side of glory. In the hymnbook God gave to his people to help them navigate life's emotions, he included an entire category of songs to sing when things are hard.

Psalms of lament give voice to our pain, anger, and frustration. While a positive attitude and outlook are powerful, and there is value in dwelling on what is good, we forfeit a great deal if we neglect to process our hardships and pain in prayer with a Father who loves us. This experience of being felt by God, or experiencing his care and attunement to us, has the power to heal us and change us, making our hard hearts soft and transforming our anger and pain into gentleness and loving-kindness.[13]

Parenting well through hardship, becoming a mom who responds instead of reacts, isn't about mental gymnastics; it's about developing a posture of dependence on a Father who loves you and who is available to you for comfort and help by the power of his Spirit.

Another way to help us process is by shedding tears, which my grandmother used to call "burping the pot." She said that in the same way that we might lift a pot lid to let steam out so that the stew won't boil over, we sometimes need to make time and space to cry so that our suppressed emotions won't blow the lid off and spill stuff all over.

After my friend's mom died, she scheduled times for herself to feel. Each time she pulled a load of warm clothes out of the dryer while her baby napped, she would lay on them and wait for the tears of anger and sorrow to come. She would have a good cry, pouring her heart out to God. And then she would stand back up and fold the laundry.

Your body and mind need to work out what you are experiencing so you won't take it out on your kids. Prayer is an important way to do this, but processing with other people, sometimes even a trusted counselor, can also be helpful. In his book *Emotionally Healthy Spirituality,* Peter Scazzero writes, "To feel is to be human. To minimize or deny what we feel is a distortion of what it means to be image bearers of our personal God. To the degree that we are unable to express our emotions, we remain impaired in our ability to love God, others, and ourselves well."[14]

So if you want to love your kids well, you need to feel your emotions instead of stuffing them, ignoring them, or wishing they didn't exist.

One Day All Will Be Made Right

"It is what it is," I said to my mom on the phone. My middle son had just thrown up, and I was coming up on a deadline. This virus had kept me from having childcare and, therefore, my much-needed work time for the past two weeks.

"Yeah," interjected my eavesdropping son. "But it's not what it will be."

"Where did you hear that?" I asked after hanging up.

"Picket says that," he responded. Picket is a character in the novel he was reading, *The Green Ember* by S. D. Smith. I'm indebted to this author for the perspective that this character provided to my son and to me. Never again will I think, "It is what it is," without thinking, "but it's not what it will be."

God is a God of redemption. Your trauma and wounds may never be fully healed on this side of eternity, but every time you bring them to God to receive comfort and care, the intimacy and safety you experience will make a difference in your heart and life.

We live with the hope that one day, all that is broken will be restored. In a conversation about childhood trauma and the hope that one day we'll be healed, my friend Aimee Joseph once joked, "I'm so excited to get my new amygdala." She was being sort of silly, but I think about that comment all the time. One day our nervous systems won't run so wild. But for now we can heed the words of Jesus: "Come to me, all you who are weary and burdened, and I will give you rest" (Matthew 11:28).

All you moms who are worn out from trying to shield yourselves from pain and tired of keeping yourselves safe, all you women whose kids are rubbing up against your raw spots, come to Jesus. Rest today in the comfort, safety, and acceptance he provides. And one day, you will enter his eternal rest. And he will wipe every tear from your eye and welcome you into his new creation, a world with no wounds and no gaps.

Let that hope fuel you as you seek to love your kids on this side of glory.

Parenting Connection

When you read a chapter about the way that our experiences affect us, your mind may go straight to the ways you suspect you're negatively affecting your kids. Later in this book, we'll talk more about what to do when you fail, but for now, let's focus for a moment on what we can do to help our kids in light of what we've learned in this chapter.

How old are your kids? That's how much (or perhaps I should say how very little) experience they have with processing the hard realities of a fallen world. It's still difficult for me sometimes as an adult. They're still relatively new here, thinking with young, under-developed brains, and they need help to learn how to process what they experience. We can help our kids develop secure attachment by being available, attentive, and attuned to them—being aware of and invested in their emotional lives. We can help them learn self-regulation by providing coregulation.[15]

When they are upset, even if it's because they've done something wrong, we can help them return their little nervous systems to a state of equilibrium by offering them a hug, singing to them, inviting them to take a deep breath with us, praying with or over them, or encouraging them to move their bodies.

You can help your kids develop the habit of responding to their own big emotions with awareness by pointing out when you see them start to become frustrated or upset, naming what you see their bodies doing, or inviting them to tell you what their bodies feel like. You can help them learn to respond with compassion by responding to *them* with compassion and empathy. I often say to my boys, "I know what it's like to feel out of control, and it doesn't feel good." Or "I'm sorry you're having a hard time right now." Or "It makes sense that this feels hard and overwhelming."

You can equip them to respond to their own emotions with curiosity by asking them the same questions that you've been encouraged to ask yourself in this chapter. You can also strive to provide a safe place for them to process, encouraging them to go to God with anything they're feeling. You can help them to depend on him by teaching them that he is compassionate, in control, and attuned to them.

Even if you feel like you still have a long way to go in your own emotional regulation, knowing the tools allows you to connect with your child when they're struggling.

Believe It for Your Motherhood

The realities of living in a fallen world shape your behavior as a mom. Rather than dismissing or minimizing the impact of your past or present hardships, be curious about how your story might be shaping the stories of your children. The hardships woven into each of our stories are never greater than the hope found in Jesus. Run to God with what you find, and receive his comfort and care. The safety and security you find there will help transform you into a mom who, rather than reacting out of self-preservation, can respond with love for God and concern for her kids.

As a father has compassion on his children,
so the LORD has compassion on those who fear him;
for he knows how we are formed,
he remembers that we are dust.
—Psalm 103:13–14

Apply It to Your Parenting

- Learn to recognize signs of dysregulation in your child and help train them to do the same by asking them what their body feels like when they're upset.
- Before correcting your child, help them return to a regulated state by taking deep breaths together, offering a hug, singing to them, or encouraging them to move their body.
- Empathize with the emotions of your child: "I know what it's like to feel ____."
- Equip your child to name their feelings and respond to their own emotions with curiosity by asking, "Hmm, I wonder why that affected me this way . . ."
- Teach your child that God is always listening and longs to hear them talk about how they feel (you can do this through instruction and by example).
- Be available, attentive, and attuned to your child—aware of and invested in their emotional life.

Part 2

Becoming the Mom You Want to Be

Chapter 5

Deciding What Needs to Change

It was one of those "why can't they just . . . ?" kind of mornings.

"Why can't they just follow the sibling conflict resolution steps so clearly displayed on the fridge?"

"Why can't they just move through their morning responsibilities without constant reminders?"

"Why can't they just do what they're asked without complaining or arguing?"

Those internal questions made their way from my mind to my mouth, the pinnacle of which was "Why can't you do anything without making a mess?" This one, prompted by the discovery of a trail of fish tank water made by one eager show-and-teller en route to the car, was followed by my insistence that *I* would carry the fish tank *myself.* Five minutes into our car ride, however, I discovered that, because I was distracted by a sibling squabble or sending someone back for socks or something, I'd left said fish tank by the door. I'd spent the five minutes leading up to that discovery ensuring that my children knew that it was their fault we were late.

Now we were *really* late.

From the U-turn until the retrieval of the tank, the Holy Spirit shifted my concerns from the faults of my children to my own. While my left hand gripped the steering wheel, my right hand made every effort to secure the tank, fish water escaping all over the center console for the entirety of the drive. An analogy I'd once heard Paul Tripp offer about a water glass came to mind. Adapted here, he might say that fishy water doesn't come out of the tank *because* it's bumped; fishy water sloshes out of that tank *when* it's bumped because the tank is filled with fishy water.[1] What spills out is what is already inside of, in Paul Tripp's language, the "causal core of your personhood."[2] Or, as Jesus pointed out, "the mouth speaks what the heart is full of" (Luke 6:45).

Parenting is a bit of a bumpy road, if you will. I thought myself a great deal holier before I became a mom. Because motherhood is exposing.

Why Do You Want to Change?

I want peace so badly, I'm willing to yell at my kids to get it.

I want everyone to get along so badly, I'll rupture relationships in pursuit of harmony.

I want calm so badly, I'm willing to create utter chaos in pursuit of it.

That's what I journaled later that afternoon as I reflected on the morning. The irony was jarring and exposing. But it also led to a helpful conclusion:

> If I worship peace, or quiet, or harmony instead of God, I'll sin to get it. I'll treat anything that threatens it as if it were an enemy, even if it's my precious children. Those good things must be

> pursued for God's sake, by the help of his Spirit, through means that don't violate his moral mandates from Scripture.

Before we can deal with the matter of what needs to change, we need to consider the motivation for change. Hating the effects of your sin (feeling like a bad mom, having a chaotic home, losing your kids' respect, etc.) will never be enough to uproot it; you'll just shift to other sinful strategies to obtain whatever it is that makes you feel like a "good mom." But how can you learn to hate sin for what it is, not for what it costs you?

We were designed to crave meaning, identity, and a sense of purpose and goodness. But because of the fall, we turn away from God and look to other things for life, worth, wholeness, and happiness. My friend Carl Laferton calls these things "not gods," and the Bible calls them "idols." Idols don't have the power to make us more like Jesus. Anything that takes the place of God in your heart can be an idol, even good things—even motherhood. If you want to experience true and lasting change, then your goal, rather than just being a "better mom" for the sake of your kids, must be to become a more Christlike mom for the glory of God. And so, before we go any further, I must caution you against making an idol out of motherhood.

We don't follow Jesus so we might be good moms; rather, we become godly moms when we follow Christ for his sake. Our eyes learn to deem "not gods" as worthless as we look longer and harder at him.

More than setting our sights on what it means to be a "good mom," we need to lift our eyes and see the beauty of Christ. As my friend Irene Sun once told me, true change is more about beholding than behaving. If your primary motivation to be different or better is anything other than the glory of Jesus, that has to be the first thing we deal with. The purification of this desire is a work that only the Spirit of God can do. Ask him to help you.

What Do You Want to Change?

You may recall from the introduction that the moms with whom I shared the title of this book as it was being written often responded with tearful confessions. These confessions usually had to do with losing their patience with their children. But this is not a book about anger specifically, and that's intentional. I don't want to dissuade you from asking God to make you a more patient and gracious mom, but I also want to challenge you to look past the anger and impatience you feel and consider other ways, maybe less obvious ways, that God may want to change you—to make you a mom who looks more like his Son.

Perhaps the most obvious problems to identify and confess in motherhood are our outward sins against our kids (like anger, impatience, or harsh words), but I would argue that the sins that pose the greatest threat to our children are the ones we don't repent of because we are either unaware of or unable to recognize them or unwilling to humble ourselves to admit them. Consider for a moment how your other subtler struggles, or more "acceptable" sins, might be leading your kids away from the heart of God: thinking or talking about others without charity or honor (comparison, envy, negativity, judgmentalism, pride), talking badly about the kids in their class or social sphere (gossip), or having a casual approach to your own sin (dismissal, blame, or lack of acknowledgment). Your kids will benefit from your willingness to take a harder look in a ruthless pursuit of holiness.

The most important person to ask about how you need to

change is God himself. As your maker, he knows who you were created to be. As the author of moral goodness, he holds the authority to say what it means to be a "good" mom. And as the only source of omniscient, perfect wisdom, he knows exactly how to get you from where you are to where he wants you to be.

So let me invite you to pause and pray before we go any further. Ask God to search your heart and see if there is any way in you that isn't of him, and ask him to lead you in his ways (Psalm 139:23–24). No, really. Pause before you read another word.

Now let's consider what change might need to take place for you to be a more Christlike mom. Try to be specific as you read and consider your own heart and experience as a mom. Hopefully, you'll be able to notice, track, and celebrate the change that God brings about within you. First, let's set some parameters for the area you choose:

1. Be Personal and Internal

This journey is about *personal* holiness. Whatever you want to change, it must be something that falls within your realm of responsibility. This means your attention needs to be devoted to what needs to change in *you*, not what needs to change in your spouse or your kids. The whole sloshed fish tank water debacle was a tragic case of being so focused on the speck in my kids' eyes that I couldn't see the log in my own.

The goal here isn't to change your behavior by changing the people around you. The goal is for you to be a mom who looks more like Jesus, even if no one around you changes one iota. And what needs to change about you isn't even the *behavior* that you fear might be ruining your kids—it's your internal motivations. The gospel gives us the cause, the courage, and the confidence to go deep, looking beyond behavior to see what it reveals about our hearts (Matthew 12:34).

Paul Tripp and Timothy Lane assert that "as much as we are affected by our broken world and the sins of others against us, our greatest problem is the sin that resides in our hearts."[3] And I would add that it is often through the sins of others and the brokenness of this world that the Lord *exposes* our hearts in order to change them as we confess our sin and receive his grace. Like the pride exposed when you feel it is beneath you to strip your child's soiled sheets, or the bitterness exposed when you miss out on something because your child spikes a fever, or the fear-of-man (people-pleasing or worshipping the opinions of others) exposed when you overcorrect your kids in public, or the hypocrisy exposed when you yell at them for the unkind tone they're using with their siblings.

When you focus on your heart instead of your circumstances or others' behavior, you become eager to see what your actions reveal about your affections—clues to what needs to change within you. This shift in focus can be marked by a shift in the language we use to think about our circumstances and our hearts. A clue that you're focusing on circumstances can be the language "if only . . .," and the shift to the words "even if" can help you to refocus on heart change instead.

Let's try a little challenge. Each time you think "if only," let it be a cue to reframe that thought by rephrasing the sentence.

Instead of:

"If only my husband were more present, then I could be the mom I want to be."

"If only my kids would just listen the first time, then I wouldn't have to be this version of myself."

"If only we had a bigger yard / separate bedrooms / more money . . ."

Try:

"Even if my husband never changes . . ."
"Even if my kids don't listen right away . . ."
"Even without more space or resources . . ."
". . . I want to be a Spirit-led, Christlike, fruitful mom. My faithfulness is not contingent on anyone else's. And God's faithfulness to change me isn't dependent on anything or anyone else changing."

The way you choose to be different should be about transforming *you* from the *inside out* for the glory of God.

2. Be Biblical and Specific

In this information age, moms are bombarded with a ton of parenting advice, perspectives, and to-dos. Many of us live under a cloud of vague "I'm a bad mom" guilt or, worse, carry around specific guilt over things that are a matter of liberty and not biblical law, like feeding your kids store-bought frozen PB&Js or sending them to a certain kind of school (or not sending them at all). And many of us even feel guilty for things we're doing right! When parenting is uncomfortable, like holding boundaries with our kids, we feel responsible for their pain when we don't give in to their deeply felt desires, but holding a boundary is actually a way to care *well* for your children!

You don't need to change your personality or adopt anyone else's persona. Again, God wants to transform you into the most

Christlike version of *you*. Be as specific as possible about what you want to change, but also be selective, letting conviction arise from *God's Word,* rather than comparison with any neighbor, social media account, or parenting book.

For example, you may be tempted to think this is what it means to be a good mom:

> A good mom reads out loud with her kids and takes them to the library. A good mom bakes with her kids. A good mom gets in the pool instead of sitting on the side of the pool. A good mom plays on the floor with her kids instead of using the moments they're playing to get stuff done. A good mom makes bread from scratch instead of buying it at the store.

Instead, redefine a good mom this way:

> A gospel-focused, godly mom is convinced of her worth rather than using her performance in motherhood to achieve her worth. A godly mom is more concerned with how her children experience her than what experiences she provides for them. A grace-filled mom sees interruptions to her own will as opportunities to do the will of God. A faithful mom takes her cues from the Word of God and not the people around her. A Christlike mom responds with self-control instead of reacting out of her flesh.

The gospel frees you from striving to be whatever you think a "good" mom is and fuels you to become a "godly" mom—one who is loving, joyful, peace-making, patient, kind, concerned with true goodness, faithful, gentle, and self-controlled.

Not everything that you want to change needs to be motherhood specific. Your kids will benefit from your pursuit of holiness in *all* aspects of life. The goal here is to become more like *Jesus*. Observe in the Gospels the way he treats people. Pay attention to the ways your character is inconsistent with his example or his explicit commands. Then prayerfully ask him to make your heart look more like his. Identify the things in your life that the Bible clearly labels as weeds, and begin the Spirit-enabled work of uprooting them from your heart so that you can bear good fruit and look more like Christ.

3. Be Hopeful

The goal here isn't just to pull weeds; it's to see you flourish as the child of God he made and rescued you to be. We're not only looking to put something to death here; we're also aiming to see life—life in the form of spiritual fruit.

The New Testament is filled with commands to "put off" behaviors that are reprehensible to God, but it also invites us to "put on" characteristics of righteousness. Don't *just* focus on the negative things you want to change; rather, envision yourself "putting on" the godly characteristics you long to possess. The process of becoming a more Christlike mom isn't a game of whack-a-mole. It's a pruning—a weeding—that gives way to a gorgeous garden.

Consider passages of Scripture where Christ perfectly modeled the characteristic you want to emulate, and use your spiritual imagination to visualize with hope how you might sound and act as a mom responds and behaves like Jesus. Then ask God to help make that a reality. Ask him to bear the fruit of the Spirit in your life, and pursue the godly characteristics that the New Testament invites you to "put on," acting like the new creation you truly are in Christ Jesus (Ephesians 4:24). Don't just think about what behavior you want to stop; think about *who you want to be*—who you were *made* to be.

For example:

I want to delight in my kids instead of trying to escape them. I want to speak kindly to my kids instead of berating them. I want to talk about and celebrate the function of bodies (mine and theirs) in front of my kids, rather than focusing on their form or shape. I want to see my children as souls to shepherd instead of problems to solve or people to fix.

Think about what your life might look like—what *you* might look like—if you were, in fact, changed. Can you picture it?

You, a mom who listens to her kids instead of shushing or dismissing them?

You, a mom who delights in her kids instead of trying to escape them?

You, a mom who uses her words to build her children up instead of tearing them down?

You, a mom who celebrates the function of her body and the bodies around her instead of being preoccupied with their form?

Sometimes when we have been struggling with a specific sin pattern for a long time, the bad behavior starts to feel inevitable. But please hear me, sister: If you are in Christ, it isn't. You have potential, so much potential, because of his presence within you! There's no room for cynicism in the heart of the believer because the same power that raised Christ Jesus from the dead is alive and at work within you. God is able to do immeasurably more than you could ever ask or imagine (Ephesians 3:20). I know the discouragement you've felt, but I want you to get super pumped about who you are becoming in Christ. God is at work. The possibilities are wildly exciting. You really can change! And you will. He loves you too much to leave you where you are.

Tracing Behaviors to Root Desires

Now that you've considered the ways you want to change, an important part of realizing that change is deciding how you will respond when those heart-exposing behaviors pop up.

We recently replaced our dryer because I was tired of having to dry every load of clothes twice for any actual drying to occur. Much to my dismay, when the new dryer arrived, it had the same problem. When I alerted my husband to this issue, he ordered a long, metal ropelike tool with a brush on the end. We attached it to a drill and sent it deeper and deeper into the dryer vent. Then he put a leaf blower in the hole and told me to go outside and watch the vent.

I heard the leaf blower turn on, then I erupted in giggles at an almost immediate eruption of lint from the outdoor vent. *Ploof.* It shot out like a cannon.

No amount of trying to fix the dryer would have made the clothes dry faster, because the problem was deeper. The same is true for us as we encounter our shortcomings. To operate according to your design and effectively do what God created you to do, you need him to work in you in much the same way as the drill-powered dryer vent brush and leaf blower.

As you examine the behavior you want to change, rather than focusing on the behavior itself, invite God to probe and reveal the deeper source of the problem—shift your attention from the "dryer" of your behavior to the "vent" of your heart. Here are some things exposed in my heart in just the last few weeks:

Once you identify the root desire behind the behavior that

Behavior	Root Desire
Ignoring my kids, not fully listening to my kids, treating my kids like an inconvenience	Love of productivity
Being inflexible and impractical, insisting on my own way	Control
Rushing my kids, fussing at them for making me late, shaming them for not cleaning up	Poor stewardship (of time, sleep, etc.)
Forcing my kids to conform to arbitrary rules, shaming them instead of claiming them when others disapprove of their behavior or appearance	Fear of man
Overcorrection, hypercriticism	Perfectionism
Putting my kids on the spot to perform so I can receive accolades or feel good about myself	Performance
Reacting harshly to something being damaged or broken instead of saying, "People are more important than things," as I've taught them	Materialism
Neglecting the work of caring for my kids and helping my kids because I'm utterly absorbed in a novel	Sloth, escapism

needs to change, bring that to God and confess it, asking him to reclaim the seat of your heart's affections. Since God is much more worthy of our affections than worldly things, a desire for him frees us from the lesser desires and affections that motivate our sinful actions. Presbyterian theologian Thomas Chalmers referred to this as "the expulsive power of a new affection."[4] Each time you see that behavior or heart attitude pop up, stop right then and there and practice repentance, pray and ask for forgiveness and help, receive his grace, and let it blow through and loosen those lesser affections hindering you from fulfilling the purpose for which you were created—helping the dryer to actually dry and helping you live a life characterized by love of God and neighbor.

When You Blow It: An Action Plan

This week I found myself feeling bad about something for several hours. I fumed in self-hatred, then I was mad at my kids for a bit, then I shifted to blaming everyone else. Finally I realized I could move from all of this guilt-fueled brooding to joy and relief if I just handled my sinful action the way that God invites me to: by turning away from the desire that motivated that action and returning to him. Repentance is how we first receive God's grace, but it's also how we access it throughout our entire lives as believers. The next time you find yourself in a similar situation, follow these four steps.

1. Trace It to the Heart

Instead of making an excuse for your behavior, view that behavior as a clue to what's going on within you. True repentance is focused not just on external actions but also on what they reveal about the heart. These behaviors signal that our hearts' affections need to be reordered. In our repentance, God changes our hearts: helping us love our kids more than our own agendas, love service more than being served, and love forgiveness more than harboring resentment. Ask yourself, "What was I loving more than God or neighbor that led me to act that way?"

2. Ask for Forgiveness

You cannot think or feel yourself into Christlikeness. Spiritual transformation is *relational,* since it is God who changes us. So instead of just knowing what you did was wrong or feeling sorry, confess your sin to God and receive his assurance of pardon. In Psalm 51:4, when David repents of sleeping with Bathsheba and murdering Uriah, he says, "Against you, you only, have I sinned." Those words need to characterize our repentance as well—not repenting because we sinned "against my pride," "against the mom I thought I'd be," or "against my kids" (although that might be true). Repentance should be motivated by godly sorrow and not just worldly regret (2 Corinthians 7:10). We should hate our sin for the affront to God that it is, not simply because of the consequences. We need to be grieved over our sin first and foremost because it breaks the heart of God, not because of the tense moments it produces, or the way it threatens the peace we long for in our homes, or the possibility that our kids might not want to be with us at holiday events when they're grown. Though the consequences of our sin can alert us to the need for change, it is a love of God, not fear of consequences, that will ultimately change us. The beauty, however, is that as we love him more, we are transformed into the moms he made us to be.[5]

3. Experience Joy and Relief

My pastor, Harrison Spitler, often reminds us that "repentance is an invitation to joy." I recite those words to myself often. In a culture so focused on being "perfect just the way you are" and "living your truth," it's not always easy to say, "What I am doing is wrong, and something about me needs to change." But it helps to remember that repentance is a *gift.* It's an opportunity to turn away from what *takes* life and turn again to the *source* of life—the God who invites us to experience joy and peace (Psalm 32). When you turn from sin, you're not just running *away* from something bad; you're running *toward* something, or rather some*one*, better.

4. Ask for God's Help

Ask the Spirit for help to fight future temptations in this area. This is the only way to defeat sin: to put the misdeeds of the flesh to death "by the Spirit" (Romans 8:13). And you can expect help from him since the Spirit makes it possible to overcome temptation by working in you and for you. He gives you the motivation to fight sin by transforming your desires (Romans 8:5), and he empowers you to fight it by interceding for you (Romans 8:27). Since the Spirit of life has set you free from the law of sin and death, you never face temptation alone and you do not have to give in to it.

You're Not on Your Own

My minivan has a feature that lets me know when I need to course correct and when I need to brake. The role of the Holy Spirit is like this. But not only does he bring guidance and conviction about what to do, he supplies believers with the power to do it. Paul wrote to the Galatians, "So I say, walk by the Spirit, and you will not gratify the desires of the flesh" (Galatians 5:16). The answer to the question "*How* do I change? How do I become the most Christlike mom version of me?" is "Live by the Spirit."

If you want to be the mom that God made you to be, walking by the Spirit is the only way to do it. Everyone who places their faith in Christ receives the Holy Spirit—our helper and advocate, the Spirit of truth who lives in us (John 14:16–18). The Spirit assures us that we are children of God, bringing us the love of the Father

(Romans 5:5) and giving us access to him (Ephesians 2:18). He also brings about faith and repentance within us, helping us to see and become more like Jesus. Living the Christian life is about depending on and drawing on the power of the Spirit of God living within you. Spiritual transformation is not a set of steps or a system, so much as a relational process.

So, what does this mean practically for you as a mom on a Tuesday morning? Because you are indwelled with the Spirit of God, you're never out of options and you're never on your own when it comes to doing what God is asking you to do. It means instead of banging the rag on the counter like Ashley Judd in *Divine Secrets of the Ya-Ya Sisterhood*, saying, "Why do I have to do everything myself?" you can lift your eyes to the source of your help and say, "I know that I am not alone, that you are with me, and that you will help me."

As you set out on this journey to become a mom who looks more like Jesus, don't think for one second that you're on your own. The same power that raised Christ Jesus from the dead is living inside you, guiding you in the truth and empowering you to live it out. Life in the Spirit is both the path and the power to change.

Each time you see the thing that you're hoping will change, repent and believe. That's the heartbeat of the Christian life: Repent and believe. Rather than you simply feeling bad and trying harder, the gospel invites you to receive grace and live more freely.

Parenting Connection

Often we make the same mistake with our kids that we make with ourselves: We focus on behavior instead of the heart. Often when our family is watching a movie, after a villain does something heinous or harmful, I'll press pause and ask, "What is that character loving or desiring?" I'll ask my kids the same question when they sin against one another. "In that moment, what were you loving or desiring more than God or neighbor?"

My goal with this question is to help them see that their actions are the overflow of their hearts. Ultimately, parenting isn't about raising well-adjusted, successful, decent human beings. The ultimate goal of parenting is to raise our kids to be people who love God with their whole selves and who love their neighbors as themselves.

Sometimes I let my desire for control or my feelings of annoyance dictate how I parent instead of living by the Spirit (in accordance with God's Word). In seasons when I find myself overcorrecting my kids, it helps to ask myself, "Is this an issue of morality or inconvenience?" "Is this behavior an affront to God and his kingdom or just to me and mine?" As we seek to help our kids own their behaviors as the overflow of their hearts, we can model this by being careful not to blame our circumstances or our kids for our own behavior. As you parent today, look past your child's behavior and aim for their heart, disciplining in a way that is both biblical and hopeful, encouraging them to keep going and to notice how God is at work in them.

From the time my kids were little, when they experienced failure, I would invite them to repent and believe. This process can be short and simple. First, I guide them in telling God sorry for what they've done, then we thank God for the forgiveness, mercy, and grace he shows us in Christ Jesus, and then we ask the Holy Spirit for help to obey. I'm hopeful that guiding my kids through this prayer in response to their failure will help them build the habit in their own lives. The repentance step cleanses their consciences; the belief step both protects them from shame and helps them remember that obedience isn't something they can or should try to conjure up on their own.

Believe It for Your Motherhood

God created and saved you for a purpose! He has a plan to change you and to use you for good, and your motherhood is a means to the end of accomplishing both of those things. He's committed to your growth and loves you too much to leave you where you are! But he's not just trying to change your behavior; he's after your heart. When your behavior exposes disordered desires within you, run to him over and over and ask him to help you love him more. This is how you'll become a more joy-filled, grace-fueled, Christlike mom.

. . . being confident of this, that he who began a good work in you will carry it on to completion until the day of Christ Jesus.
—Philippians 1:6

Apply It to Your Parenting

As you read books, watch movies, or go about your day, train your kids to see behavior as an indication of what's going on inside:

- "What is that character loving or desiring?"
- "In that moment, what were you loving or desiring more than God or neighbor?"

Help them to build the habit of depending on God's grace to cleanse their conscience, protect them from shame, and motivate their obedience by responding to their failure with these steps:

- telling God sorry for what they've done
- thanking God for the forgiveness, mercy, and grace he shows us in Christ Jesus
- asking the Holy Spirit for help to obey

Chapter 6

Abiding in Christ (Prayer and Scripture)

Yesterday was a momentous day. My youngest child successfully learned to wipe his own bottom. I rejoiced the day that everyone was toilet trained (goodbye, diaper bag!), when everyone could eat on their own and dress themselves, and when everyone was able to buckle themselves in the car. And I have longed for the day when no one would shout, "Come wipe me!" And now (though, admittedly, we still need to work on remembering to flush) that day is here. I often joke that my goal in motherhood is to work myself out of a job. But our relationship with God is not like this. We were never meant to do it on our own.

The goal of the Christian life is not independence; it's *de*pendence. Jesus articulates this with the metaphor of a vine and branches, saying, "If you remain in me and I in you, you will bear much fruit; apart from me you can do nothing" (John 15:5). We were never meant to outgrow him. If dependence is the goal of the Christian life, then the expression of faithful dependence is a reliance on God through both prayer and Scripture, communicating with God and hearing from him.

First, let's explore prayer. Your prayer life is the most accurate measure of your dependence on Jesus. Think about the last time you thought, "I can't do this!" What happened next? Was it prayer?

"I Can't Do This" Versus "I've Got This"

In Mark 9, when the disciples asked Jesus why they couldn't heal a boy with an unclean spirit, Jesus's response reveals that they had become self-reliant. After tasting success in ministry, they had slipped into an "I've got this" mentality.

The conversation they had before this event revealed that they underestimated their need for a Savior. The conversation they had with Jesus after the event reveals that they also underestimated the magnitude of the task before them, overestimating their own abilities. Moreover, we see that the father of the boy overestimated the evil that had taken his son captive and underestimated the willingness of Christ to bring restoration. Jesus invited all of them to make him their reference point and to depend on him. And he's asking you to do the same in motherhood.

Pause to assess your perspective, both on the change God is working in you and on the work he has called you to with the little people in your care.

Are you aware of your need for a Savior, or do you dismiss it or explain it away?

Are you aware of what needs to change in you and that only Jesus can change it, or do you rely on controlling external factors and regimenting your life?

If you struggle to pray, is it because you overestimate your own abilities or underestimate the problem?

Is there any indication that you become cynical, underestimating God's concern or capability for what you're currently facing as a mom?

Or maybe you're self-reliant, underestimating your need for help to deal with the hard stuff inside and around you, because you cope by muscling through?

As you seek to change and to parent well as a work in progress, you must regularly and routinely make God your reference point and adopt a posture of faithful dependence. Prayer reorients our hearts to God's capability, his concern, and his power over everything we face in motherhood. So how do we cultivate the habit of reorienting our hearts and connecting to God's power to do the work he has called us to with our kids?

The Practice of Prayer

A set-aside time for prayer functions as sort of a daily check-in that reorients my heart to both the source of my help and the mission of my life. Dedicated prayer time changes our hearts as it shapes our concerns. But if you're anything like me, when you start to pray, before long, you're thinking about your grocery list or to-do list. This doesn't mean you're bad at prayer; it just means you're human. We all need a little help to focus, and a template can provide just that. Thankfully, Jesus gave us one in the Lord's Prayer in Matthew 6. Many mentors and pastors have recommended praying through this prayer, and I love to use it to begin my personal worship time.

I use the acronym PARCA to follow the template of the Lord's

Prayer. (You're welcome for the image of prayer as a fluffy down jacket. I hope you'll never forget it.)

Praise
Align
Request
Confess
Anticipate

1. **Praise:** *Our Father in heaven, hallowed be your name.*

   Start by "hallowing" God's name. Just praise him for who he is, not for what he does for you. List his attributes and lavish praise on him.
2. **Align:** *Your kingdom come, your will be done, on earth as it is in heaven.*

   Pray for God's purposes to be accomplished in your life, the life of your family, and the lives of those around you. This is the part where you bring your desires under his, acknowledging his purposes to be higher than yours and aligning your concerns with his.
3. **Request:** *Give us today our daily bread.*

   Ask God for the things you need. You can also intercede for other people during this part, asking for what they need.
4. **Confess:** *And forgive us our debts, as we also have forgiven our debtors.*

   Ask him to search your heart and reveal any affections that are out of order. Reflect on your actions and confess sins, asking for forgiveness and the power to change.
5. **Anticipate:** *And lead us not into temptation, but deliver us from the evil one.*

   Anticipate the temptation you will face today and ask for God's help, praying that he will bear fruit in your life and help you to honor him.

This practice could be done in the morning, but it doesn't have to be. It could happen at naptime or just before bed. It could be aloud or written out in a journal. It could last for five minutes or an hour. It could happen in the car, prompted by a notecard taped to your steering wheel. The important thing is that you set aside regular, daily time to communicate with God. This helps to reset your priorities, relieve you of the feeling that everything is up to you, remind you of your life purpose, and reconnect you with your Father.

You Have 24/7 Access to the Father

Do you have "favorites" in your phone contacts? I just rely on my recent call list. These are the people I call or text most often. And sometimes I'm quicker to text one of these people to ask for prayer than I am to pray myself. Or I'm quicker to call on one of them than I am to call on God.

A few months ago, one of my kids started screaming and crying every time we sat down to do his math worksheet. I found myself getting anxious about it every day. Philippians 4:6–7 urges us to process our anxiety in prayer, asking for what we need and thanking God for his help: "Do not be anxious about anything, but in every situation, by prayer and petition, with thanksgiving, present your requests to God. And the peace of God, which transcends all understanding, will guard your hearts and your minds in Christ Jesus." Any anxiety we experience in motherhood should always be a cue to pray. Anytime we feel out of control, we can run to the One who is always in control. Nehemiah offers us a great example of this.

Upon hearing of the destruction of the wall of Jerusalem, the burning of the gates, and the hardship of Jews in Judah, Nehemiah sat down and wept. After weeping, he fasted and prayed for several *months*. Then Nehemiah got an opportunity to ask the king for permission to go and help. The king asked what he wanted, and before he answered, Nehemiah paused to pray (Nehemiah 2:4–5). His life beautifully illustrates the practice of honest prayers of lament, persistent prayers of preparation, and spontaneous prayers of supplication (or help).

Here's what those prayers can look like in the context of motherhood:

1. Honest Prayers of Lament

At a baby shower, I once objected to someone telling an expecting mother to "enjoy every moment," commenting, "Well, not every moment is enjoyable, actually." Some aspects of motherhood are unimaginably hard, and the Bible is incredibly honest about the hardship of life on this side of glory. In fact, in his Word God gives us songs of lament to give voice to our pain, anger, and frustration. When we know God is listening, prayer can work in much the same way that talk therapy does, giving us a safe place to process emotions, thoughts, and feelings, to let out anger, and to seek comfort and help. In the case of the math-associated screaming, my lament often sounded like, "God, I hate this screaming thing. It hurts my ears, it's confusing, and it's overstimulating. I want it to stop."

2. Persistent Prayers of Preparation

Before my son and I would start the math worksheet, I would pray a prayer that sounded like this: "Father, I can expect that my son will scream when we sit down to do his math today. I need your help, Lord. When that moment comes, will you help me to remain calm and to respond from a Spirit-led place instead of in a reactive way? I want to model self-control for my son, and I want to focus on helping him develop self-regulation skills instead of raising my voice to try to control the situation. Please help me. Amen." Prayers like this, which can be prayed during a set-apart prayer time or anytime before an anticipated hardship, not only help us prepare mentally but also invite God's help, which changes the way we show up.

3. Spontaneous Prayers of Supplication

In high school my sisters and I loved watching the spy show *Alias*. In each episode, the operatives would sit around a table getting all the details of a mission before going out, but once they were in the field, they wouldn't stop communicating with their handlers—they had cool earpieces that kept them connected.

Similarly, there's no need for you to live the mission of the Christian life as if the comms are down. God's Word instructs us to "pray continually" (1 Thessalonians 5:17). This means we can communicate with God in the lengthier, daily, disciplined way we just talked about, but we can also communicate with him with what I like to refer to as "walkie-talkie" or "earpiece" prayers when we're doing the "fieldwork" of motherhood: kneeling by the bathtub, buckling the car seat, pushing the stroller, administering an icky-tasting medicine, trying to finish cooking dinner with a kid tugging our shirt hem, or helping with homework.

We are never helpless, because we can always appeal to God for help in the moment. He always hears. He always helps. Spontaneous prayer is the ultimate earpiece prayer—something you can reach for in overwhelming, overstimulating, frustrating, or defeating moments of motherhood instead of just reacting out of those emotions. For example, in the math scenario, I might place a hand on my screaming son and ask God to calm him. I might also place my hands over my eyes or head and spontaneously pray (sometimes out loud) that God would protect this child from my anger and fill me with love and patience. But spontaneous prayer can take many forms.

- Spontaneous Intercession: When we feel powerless to help our kids, we can appeal to God through prayers of **intercession** for them right there on the spot. During this math drama, I prayed for my son, "Father, help him to feel able to do the work you set before him. Give him a sound mind and self-control."
- Spontaneous Prayers of Reflection: Prayer can invite God's searching of us. You can take a moment of **reflection** when you're tempted to react. "Lord, what is it in me that is so angered by this struggle my son is having? A desire for control? A love of efficiency? A longing to feel good about myself as an educator? Show me where I'm putting anything before you, and help me to love you more."
- Spontaneous Prayers of Repentance: When we blow it, prayer can take the form of **repentance**. "God, I sinned against you and against my child when I lost my temper with him just now. Please forgive me and help me to love you and love him more than I love my comfort or control." You don't have to carry a guilty conscience around until your next scheduled prayer time. You can pray right when you blow it—right there in front of your kids. And the grace you receive fuels your obedience.
- Spontaneous Prayers of Gratitude: As Philippians 4 suggests, prayer can also take the form of **gratitude**. Regularly affirming and acknowledging the kindness of God protects us from growing suspicious of him. We can thank him for all he has given us in Christ, for little things we love about nature, for

aspects of our children that delight us (hello, summertime freckles), and especially for ways that he is faithful to answer prayers for help in our time of need. Giving him the glory for our successes protects us from the very pride and self-reliance that keep us from praying.

Prayer grows us in our awareness of our dependence on God, thereby protecting us from the temptation toward self-sufficiency.

A Posture of Dependence

If the word *desperate* in the subtitle of this book resonated with you, you're in a perfect position to cultivate a healthy prayer life, dependent on God to help you and to change you.

Even if you don't know what to say, Scripture assures us that the Spirit of God intercedes for us with groanings too deep for words (Romans 8:26). Turn your shame heavenward. Turn your confusion heavenward. Turn your doubts heavenward. Turn your desires heavenward. And as you ask for God's help, you'll start to see it more and more. The goal isn't to get rid of that feeling of desperation; it's to aim it heavenward to eradicate discouragement. The other beautiful thing about this conversation with God, though, is that it isn't one-sided.

Hearing from God Through Scripture

When I had a three-year-old and a six-month-old, I didn't get much sleep. The six-month-old woke up at 4:30 every morning. And if I didn't get there quickly enough, so would his brother. So I would bring the six-month-old with me to the other side of the house to protect the sleep of everyone else. While he mastered the art of sitting up, patted the floor, chewed on toys, and kicked on his play mat, I wished I were sleeping and resented his being awake.

Then one day I heard someone say that in one year, you can read through the entire Bible in just twelve minutes a day. So I decided to use a portion of the morning to read the Bible. I started in Genesis. Every day, I wrote the date, the time, and the chapter of the Bible I was in and recorded what the passage revealed about God.

In those early mornings, sometimes my eyes didn't focus so well, so I'd follow along with the audio from a Bible app. Sometimes I'd listen to the audio while I played with the baby, occasionally crawling over to underline something or put a question mark by something I didn't understand. Eventually, the baby started crawling too. Before long, my quiet reading time became a shared adventure, with his chubby, grippy fingers ripping a few pages out of my Bible during this season. When he turned one, he started grabbing board books and toddling over to read beside me. Gradually, I stopped resenting this time and began to look forward to it. I was in awe of the connections I was making between the Old and New Testaments and the uncanny (dare I say providential?) connections between what I was reading and my own life. I started to feel as if I needed the Bible more than I needed breakfast.

When my third baby was six months, it wasn't like this at all. I struggled mentally, and for months I could only read the Psalms. And I read them more sporadically than routinely, leaving my Bible open on the counter. I wasn't spiritually hungry, but I knew I needed nourishment, and the Lord sustained me.

Now, with a nine-, seven-, and almost five-year-old, I'm able to wake up before my kids to read. But there have been weeks, even seasons, when I have read the Bible during their afternoon quiet time, or just listened to Bible songs with the boys in the car, or read the sermon text for that week over and over because focusing on anything else felt too hard. My Bible reading routine and method of Scripture intake have looked different in every season, but what hasn't changed is my need for the Word of God and for its power. How have I seen that power in my life? The Word of God has

- called me out of self-pity into selfless service,
- moved me to love when I was tempted to resent my husband,
- prompted me to forgive when I felt entitled to hatred,
- reminded me of the needs of the poor when I was consumed with my own unfulfilled desires,
- comforted me in sorrow, protecting me from bitterness,
- helped me to see the beauty and glory of Jesus when my own way seemed better,
- provided me with parenting wisdom as I learned from the family history contained within it,
- encouraged me to persevere when I lacked faith and endurance, and
- pointed me to the truth when I believed lies.

The author of Hebrews acknowledges the power of this book, using the descriptors "alive" and "active" (Hebrews 4:12). Commenting on this verse, Michael Kruger, a New Testament scholar, writes, "The word of God . . . doesn't just say things; it does things. It is busy working, changing, building, convicting, encouraging, exposing, rebuking, giving light and wisdom, carving out the path of our lives, and showing us the truth of God."[1]

Why Is It So Hard to Read the Bible as a Mom?

You don't need a list of what makes it hard to read the Bible when you have kids at home. But beyond a constantly changing schedule and endless interruptions (that don't stop when the sun goes down), I wonder if our unrealistic expectations make reading the Bible feel harder than it has to be. It doesn't have to be thirty minutes with a candle and a commentary. It doesn't have to happen at a certain time of day. It just needs to happen. Engaging with God's Word during motherhood, like anything else we try to accomplish as moms, requires creativity and adaptability.

It's been said that necessity is the mother of invention, and ultimately, to overcome the obstacles to reading the Bible in motherhood, we need to be utterly convinced that it's something we need. I suspect that the reason moms don't read the Bible is that we are not persuaded of its power and potential in our lives. So let's take a moment to remember and reflect on that power and potential:

- Scripture is how we remain in and enjoy the love of Jesus (John 15:1–8).
- God speaks to us through his Word, revealing himself and his will for us (2 Timothy 3:16).
- The Bible goes beneath the surface and symptoms, exposing what is inside us. It sifts through our outward behavior to expose our inward desires or our disordered loves (Hebrews 4:12).
- Scripture provides nourishment for our hungry souls (Deuteronomy 8:3).
- Meditating on and memorizing Scripture is an effective strategy to fight sin (Psalm 119:10–11).

In John 15:7, Jesus tells his followers that the key to bearing fruit is abiding in him and letting the Word of God dwell in our hearts, thereby informing our actions. The key ingredient to forming Christlike character and to bearing fruit in motherhood is the Word of God. There is no substitute. When we believe this, we let go of expectations and excuses and instead think creatively about how to engage with God's Word.

When and How to Study the Bible

You're a mom, so it's pretty much a given that you've got a million things going on, any of which could be derailed by the stomach bug at any moment. If it's hard to find time to even eat lunch, when are you supposed to fit in studying an ancient text that sometimes feels irrelevant and hard to understand?

If you already have a routine that works for you, that's great! But if you still can't figure out how and when to read the Bible, I recommend what I call the 3–5 method. This is what I used when my boys were newborns or experienced sleep regressions, and it's what I use during seasons of transition. Why the name? In this method, you study three to five verses at a time for three to five minutes at a time.

The 3–5 Method

- Choose a book of the Bible. This way, you can learn the context, author, and audience of the book, and all the verses you read will be in that context (if you're able to invest in a study Bible, all this information will be inside it!). I recommend starting with one of the gospels (Matthew, Mark, Luke, John) or an epistle (any of the letters in the New Testament).

- Find a time in your day (and maybe some backups) when you can expect to have three to five minutes of concentration. If this feels tricky, try to think of a time of day when you find yourself scrolling on your phone. Try the first three to five minutes after you put your child down for a nap, or the first moments of the day when you find yourself alone, or a stretch when your kids usually play independently. You can even put your Bible in your bathroom if that's the only place you get three to five minutes to yourself. Set a timer if you want to ensure your ability to focus for this small chunk of time.
- Begin with a prayer that God would help you to focus and that the Holy Spirit would give you wisdom, understanding, and patience.
- Use the first day to study the context, author, intended audience, and themes of the book you've chosen (you can find this info online at blueletterbible.com).
- After the initial day, devote three to five minutes to the reading and study of three to five verses each day. If it needs to be two minutes or six minutes on any given day, that's okay. This method isn't meant to be rigid, just realistic.
- After you read the verses, look up words you don't know, or read a different translation if something seems confusing. Jot down questions you might have or things you want to think more about.
- Then use this framework to engage with those few verses:
    - **Observe (What does it say?)** Do you see any repeated words? Transition words? Does anything stand out?
    - **Interpret (What does it mean?)** What does this verse say about God? About people? About Jesus?

- **Apply (How should I live?)** How does what these verses say about God, humanity, or the subject it addresses apply to your own life? What is this passage calling you to believe with your mind? What is it asking you to love with your heart? What is it instructing you to do with your hands or life?
- When your three to five minutes are up, get up without guilt, having nourished your soul and gained something to meditate on for the rest of the day. If another pocket of time emerges in your day—maybe while your kids are playing or you're waiting for water to boil during dinner prep—feel free to do another three to five minutes.[2]

The Value of Group Study

During the school year, my personal Bible study is determined by what the women's Bible study at church is studying. If you're not in one already, I highly recommend joining a Bible study (not a *book* study). The Bible was written to be read and studied collectively, so studying the Bible with other people is a great way to learn. I'm always grateful for the insights that other women provide, and discussing God's Word helps it to sink deeper into my heart. Studying the Bible with women in other stages of life has impacted my relationship with my kids over and over again as the text becomes more memorable and more clearly applicable. As we discuss the passage, I also glean from the insight of other women. Not only am I trained in the art of application by listening to theirs, but I am helped as I share life with them because they also use Scripture to speak into what they know of my life.

As you listen to other women (who may be less sleep deprived than you) apply the Word to their lives, you'll learn to apply it to yours. And as you share more of your lives together, maybe they'll even help you apply it to your specific situation too.

If your local Bible study day and time don't work for you or there's no childcare, consider asking an older woman to read through a book of the Bible with you. You could text about it or meet up once a week and read in real time while your kids run around.

Sunday mornings are another great setting to study and learn the Bible. My pastors teach through a book at a time (we've been in Genesis for months), and at the end of a sermon series, my knowledge of that book of the Bible is so much greater and my personal study of that book is forever enriched.

Don't Forget to Eat

Moms are the most creative and resourceful people I know. You are a problem-solver by nature and practice. If you can figure out when and how to feed yourself and your kids with an always-changing and often-interrupted schedule (hello, car seat blowout), you can figure out when and how to study the Bible.

Sometimes it might look like shoving a granola bar in your mouth (studying a few verses at a time).

Sometimes it might be eating a Gatorade gel pack on the run (listening to an app on the go).

Sometimes it might look like sharing a long, leisurely meal with friends (group Bible study).

Sometimes it might be eating Goldfish with your kids (memorizing simple verses with them or listening to kids' Bible songs in the car).

And sometimes it looks like a glorious lunch by yourself (thirty minutes of study time with a journal and a Bible highlighter and a gel pen . . . maybe just don't mention it to the sleep regression mom, okay?).

All Bible intake counts, and all of it serves you. I've memorized a *lot* of Scripture without even trying by listening to songs from Seeds Kids Worship and Slugs and Bugs with my boys. Recently, when reading a chunk of text from Isaiah, I found myself singing a Slugs and Bugs tune I learned during a ride in the minivan.

Moms don't live on food alone but on every word that comes from the mouth of God. The Bible is your sustenance, my friend. The most important thing is that you don't *not* eat, either because you don't think you need food or because you think you don't have time for it. Get creative. Find a way to make the Bible a part of your daily life. As you do, you'll see the beauty of God more clearly. As your affection for Christ and awe of God grow, so will your disdain for sin. And that will transform your experience of motherhood and your kids' experience of you.

Abiding in Christ

I talked with my sister the other day—you know, the one whose son had open heart surgery—and she said she's felt a major shift within herself recently. She's done a lot of courageous work in counseling, but this shift, she relayed, has come about through a renewed commitment to reading the Word of God and to daily prayer and communion with God. She's convinced of the Bible's power in her life, telling me, "This has been a game changer. I see a marked difference in the way I interact with my kids as a result of reading the Bible and praying and truly believing that God is with me and for me."

Jesus is abundantly clear that the only path to fruitful motherhood is abiding in him, and Jamison's testimony confirms it. Do you want your motherhood to be fruitful? Characterized by love, joy, peace, patience, kindness, goodness, gentleness, faithfulness, and self-control? Remain in him through prayerful communication, and let his words remain in you through your regular intake of Scripture, and you *will* bear much fruit.

Parenting Connection

Most days, before my husband leaves for work and the boys and I leave for the gym, our family prays. It's not complicated. And it takes less than five minutes. We take turns asking and answering, "How do you need God's help today?" I especially love hearing my kids intercede for one another—and for their mom and dad. Here are a few of our most recent ones: This morning one of my boys asked for prayer that God would help him not let his feelings tell him what to do. One of them asked for patience with his brothers. One of them asked for prayer that he would not provoke his brothers. I've asked the boys to pray that God would help me love them more than I love being on time. This morning my husband David asked us to pray that he would be diligent and trust God with his work. Sometimes the brothers add little bits to the requests: "And please help him to love his brothers more than his Legos today. Amen." Or "God, please help him to have self-control and not scream."

Beginning our days this way cultivates a posture of dependence on God. I never want my kids to think that obedience is something they have to conjure up on their own, and I always want them to know that God's help is available to them. They know they can't do anything apart from him, and this exercise reinforces that. When we put them to bed at night, we often reflect on their request from that morning. This gives us opportunities to celebrate as we see God answer prayers and grow us in his grace!

Your kids will learn the importance of prayer as you pray with, over, and for them. Similarly, as they see you valuing God's Word, they'll learn to value it as well. When my oldest was two, he would grab his storybook Bible and flip through its pages while I did my personal worship time with my own Bible in my lap. Since God works through his Word, if we want to see him work in the lives of our kids, we need to expose them to it. One of the most loving things we can do for them is to help store up his truth in their hearts and minds. The important thing is that your kids know that the Bible is where God reveals who he is, who we are, what his plans are, and what he has to say to us. It's where we go for guidance, answers, comfort, to learn what is right and wrong, and to hear the good news of the gospel.

Over the years our Bible study has taken on different forms. We have listened to Bible songs in the car together (the beat and quality matter—check out Slugs and Bugs, Seeds Kids Worship, or Shai Linne); we have done memory challenges; we have daily read a story out of a picture Bible; we have read from the Tales That Tell the Truth series; we've gone through Susan Hunt's *My ABC Bible Verses*. But no matter the specific format we're using, we reference the Bible as we go throughout our day and have conversations about the issues we're facing. I'll often ask my kids, "What does God's Word have to say to us about this?" They can draw from all the stories and songs we've done to apply what they've learned.

My husband and I have also chosen to join a church that has a high view of Scripture, and we're committed to getting the boys to their age-appropriate Sunday school classes, where they are being taught to understand the stories of the Bible within the bigger story of redemption. Just as with meals, we can't force them to eat, but we can be faithful to set God's Word in front of our kids.

If talking about the Bible with your kids is intimidating, remember that you don't need to have it all figured out. When they have questions you don't know the answers to, you can model humility and the willingness to learn, saying, "Let's figure that out together." You can talk with your pastor or ask someone a bit farther along on their journey. It's never too late to start opening God's Word with your kids and talking about it. I'm pausing to pray that as you do, you'll be delighted by what you experience.

Believe It for Your Motherhood

You can't produce spiritual fruit by trying harder. And you can't conjure it up by gritting your teeth or squeezing your eyes shut and willing yourself to be more Christlike. Spiritual fruit is the byproduct of abiding in Christ, communing with him by letting his Word dwell in you richly and remaining tethered to him in a prayerful posture of dependence. The spiritual disciplines of prayer and Bible study are God's chosen instruments to make you more like Jesus—because being with him and beholding him is a transformational experience. Abide in the true vine and watch for the fruit.

Remain in me, as I also remain in you. No branch can bear fruit by itself; it must remain in the vine. Neither can you bear fruit unless you remain in me.

—John 15:4

Apply It to Your Parenting

- Play Scripture songs in the car or in your home.
- Make a habit of reading storybook Bibles to help your kids grasp the big story of redemption and God's heart for people.
- Whenever possible, reference Scripture when talking to your kids about the way we interact with the world and others.
- Talk to your kids about what you're reading and learning in God's Word.
- Make a habit of praying with your kids at transitions (before moving to the next activity or getting out of the car).
- Find five minutes every day when you can gather and ask, "How do you need God's help?" and pray for one another as a family.
- Thank God when you see something beautiful or experience something good.
- Pause and pray in front of your kids when you're overwhelmed or are acutely aware of your need.

Chapter 7

Sharing Life with Others (Community)

"Hi, I'm not doing awesome."

I tapped Send.

A few moments later, my college roommate Jenny's photo popped up on my vibrating phone. I answered her call and immediately launched into telling her what was hard about this afternoon, this season, and the moments leading up to my SOS text. "This is really hard, Abbey," she comforted me. I told her the humiliating detail that had me wondering if I belonged in the loony bin. Jenny said it made a lot of sense. I talked about the actions I regretted. No, it wasn't okay, she agreed, but she reminded me that yes, it was redeemable.

Then Jenny restored me to the truth I so desperately needed to hear: that I am human. That God's power is made perfect in weakness. That Christ's work covers my failures with grace. That one hard afternoon doesn't negate all the good work God is doing in and through me. She also told me a mortifying moment she'd had with her five-year-old that day. "I'm so sorry I'm laughing," I snorted through my tears to this dear friend who had just become the victim of my emotional whiplash. "Oh, I think we probably should laugh," she graciously responded. Then laugh we did about the absurdity of motherhood. She prayed over me before we ended the call.

This exchange with Jenny drove a spoke into the wheel of my doomsday bike ride down a shame spiral. It turned my whole day around, moved my heart to praise, and led to a redemptive evening with my boys.

I recently was on the other end of an exchange like this. I reminded a friend running on little sleep that even if she'd had a rough night and missed her morning time with the Lord, God still had good works for her to walk in and the Holy Spirit was still living inside her (my text included that arm flexing emoji). We strategized about how she might practically handle the demands of the day with her little kids.

Both of these exchanges made me a better mom. Both of them underscored this truth: It takes a village. This is often said in the context of raising a child, but God's design to grow *you* up into a spiritually mature, Christlike mom also requires a whole host of others. Spiritual transformation is a group project. God transforms us not only through prayer and his Word but also through our relationships with others.

For those embedded in Western culture, our approach to change tends to be extremely individualistic and narrowly focused, like it's just us and Jesus. But when you became a Christian, you were saved into a family, the plural "people" for whom Christ gave his life (Titus 2:14). God intends for the life of the Christian—your life as a believing mom—to be lived out in the context of relationships with other believers. As members of Christ's body, we belong to one another; we *need* one another (Romans 12:4–5). By God's design, participation in community life and the local church is essential to Christian maturity. There's no other way to become the mom God saved you to be than in the context of Christian community.

Community Offers Help and Support

One of the most moving lines I've ever read came from J. R. R. Tolkien's *The Lord of the Rings: The Return of the King.* The main character, Frodo Baggins, has been assigned the task of destroying a ring. But as he climbs Mount Doom, burdened by the weight of the Ring and weary from a difficult journey, Frodo collapses, unable to continue. His trusted and loyal companion Samwise Gamgee bends to pick him up. "Come, Mr. Frodo," he says to his friend. "I can't carry it for you, but I can carry you and it as well."[1] Frodo could not have completed the journey on his own, and he was never intended to. By saving you into a family, God provides you with the help and support you need to do the work he has called you to. You were never meant to do motherhood alone.

One of the primary ways we experience God's love and care is through his people. This can be immensely practical. When our second baby died in my womb, my friend Maggie showed up to clean my house. Our friends Joe and Christine brought takeout. Women from my church played with my son so that I could have time and space to grieve and heal and go to doctor's appointments. When my back went out a few weeks later, my friend Anne showed up at every nap transition to lift my toddler in and out of his crib. This is the family of God in action.

God has used his people time and time again to meet my needs or help me to keep going when I felt too weak to continue. And sometimes my community has helped to lighten my load by recommending that I set something down, calling attention to my need for rest or margin when I've been ignoring the cues to slow down.

How Do We Get This Kind of Community?

God designed us to share life with others, but what he has offered in principle isn't always there in practice. As you read about how people showed up for me in that season of pregnancy loss, maybe you felt a deficit or lack of support. I've waded through my own fair share of disappointment within this body of believers, even with some of the very people I mentioned, actually. But community is something you must *pursue*, moving toward others and showing up for gatherings, events, and conversations. Loving others is one way you can help foster the community you want to have.[2]

Community is something you *prioritize* when you look for a church home and plan your calendar. If you want to become the mom God made you to be, community must be a priority.

Community is something you *pray* for, asking God to provide for you and then expectantly being on the lookout for his provision.

Community is something we have to *pay attention to*, because if we're not looking for it, we'll miss it. Overwhelm can cause me to feel isolated and helpless. Just like I forget all our outing options on a rainy day, I often forget community in my time of need. For me, it has been helpful to make a list of people who are available to help and support me and keep it accessible for when needs arise.

Take a moment to grab a pencil and paper or open the notes app on your phone, and make a list of any people who have ever said, "Let me know if you need anything," or with whom you feel safe or comfortable asking for help. Next time you're overwhelmed or have a tough week or evening, pull out this list and give someone the opportunity to come alongside you.

Community is also something you must *participate* in, allowing others to show up for you but also supporting others when their needs arise. Take a moment to make another list, one of people you can serve within your local body of believers. How can you come alongside them, even with limited time and mental energy? Maybe it's just by providing prayer or encouragement, or offering to grab something for them next time you're at the store, or snagging one of their kids for a playdate to give them some margin.

If this kind of love and service doesn't characterize your local body, this might be a reason to look for a different community. But before you jump ship, remember you're not just meant to be a recipient of community; you're also a *part* of that family. You can love people into being the community you long for.

In sharing life with others, you not only receive support from others but also help to bear their burdens, which God uses to make *you* holier. As you serve and consider the needs of others, God delivers you from selfishness and helps you grow in love of neighbor, which makes you a better mom to your littlest neighbors.

Create Opportunities to Be with Other Moms

Every Thursday night during the summer, we gather at the beach with a bunch of families to share picnic meals and coparent. As I build sandcastles with my friends' kids and watch other dads teach my kids to surf or see my husband pulling their kids on boogie boards, my heart swells with a sense of mission, purpose, and belonging. Can you create a regular time of connection like this?

Maybe you can meet at a park or gather for a family kickball game. If your schedule is busy, what are you already doing that you might welcome someone else to join in on? Going to the park? The library? Doing life with others doesn't have to be complicated, but as the Healthy Mind Platter showed us and God's Word affirms, we need to be with others. And you might bless another mom by inviting her to join you.

Several weeks ago, I met a few other moms at Chick-fil-A so that we could coparent while our husbands were all out of town or working late. When my kids were younger, my friend Rebecca and I prayed for each other that we would display the fruits of self-control and patience as we showed up solo to bedtimes in our respective homes when our husbands had elder meetings. We would check in with each other afterward via text. If one of us had blown it, we'd preach the gospel to the other. And if it went well, we'd praise God together and celebrate with each other. Sometimes on nights when my husband is gone, I'll invite a single mom and her kids over. Whether you're married and solo parenting is an occasional occurrence, or you're single and solo bedtimes are your norm, you can reach for this same sort of accountability and encouragement by offering or asking for it.

Coparenting with other moms not only eases the burden but also helps me to remember that I'm fun. Sharing life with my community helps me access parts of myself that I don't experience as readily in isolation or, sadly, when I'm alone with my kids. When I play with my friends' kids or serve in kids' ministry, I access the dormant camp counselor inside me and become more playful and engaged with my own children.

Spending time with other moms can also be more formal. For three years starting around the time my third son was born,

I met weekly with a group of moms to pray for each other, study God's Word, and hold one another accountable. We signed a covenant saying we were willing to ask and to be asked hard questions. We confessed to one another and offered each other support and accountability. Those three years were some of the most transformational years of my life, and each of those women would say the same. There was no hiding, and so there was flourishing.

Find an Older Woman to Teach You and Offer Wise Counsel

Once, after listening to me complain for a good twenty minutes about how my husband was never home for dinner, my older mom friend Holly, whose husband travels for work, kindly asked, "Where in the Bible does it say he has to be home for dinner?"

Holly was committed to helping me walk in obedience, prioritizing God's Word above my feelings. Rather than pointing a finger at me, she held up Scripture like a mirror, leading me to repentance, not resentment. She called me to assume the attitude of Christ in every situation—to set aside my desire for comfort and prioritize instead my desire for God's glory in my life and marriage.

Does it feel good to get this kind of advice? Of course not. Our ears long to hear that we are excused from obedience and that our desire to gratify the knee-jerk reactions of our flesh is valid. But the goal of wise counsel is our holiness. Wise counsel asks us to love the people around us rather than punish or manipulate them. It seeks God's glory over personal comfort. It seeks our sanctification over our gratification. I've learned so much by watching Holly. I've read to my kids the books she read with hers, used the resources she's recommended, and emulated her parenting.

Is there an older woman in your community you can ask to share life with you and offer wise counsel? This process doesn't have to be formal. It doesn't even have to be on a consistent schedule. Consider approaching an older woman at your church and saying, "I'd like to learn from you." See what she offers.

Share Your Story with Others

My watch vibrated on my wrist with a high heart rate notification. In the small group that David and I were a part of, we were taking turns sharing our stories, and that week it was my turn. As I reached a certain point in my story, my heart pounded and my voice quivered. But I noticed that the eyes of the men and women in this circle, rather than narrowing in judgment, filled with tears. The veins in our teacher friend Dylan's temple bulged as he tightened his jaw and clenched his fists in anger over what had been done to me in a school setting. When I finished, his tear-filled eyes looked at mine. "I'm sorry for what happened to you. And I'm angry about it too."

Dylan's mixed reaction of anger and compassion, mingled with the responses of the other people in that room, healed something in me that night. That room of individuals became a collective of compassionate witnesses to my trauma. Their empathetic reactions changed the way I told that story to myself and others from that point on. Today, I can tell that part of my story without any physical symptoms of anxiety. But beyond that, I see a difference in the way I respond to my son when he displays certain behaviors. Instead of reacting out of my own trauma, ironically trying to shame him out of those behaviors to shield him from what I believe they led me to experience as a kid, I can shepherd him because I now have compassion, not contempt, for the little girl in my story. I love my son better and am better able to be the person I want to be in his story because my community loved and listened to mine. Community has the power to help you parent as a healed mom.

As you know, our past suffering can impact our present behavior as parents. We are wounded in the context of relationship with others, but we are also healed in the context of relationship with others—and that healing shows up in our interactions with our kids. From a neuroscientific perspective, psychologist and Christ follower Curt Thompson writes, "Remember, there is no such thing as an individual brain. Transformation requires a collaborative interaction, with one person empathically listening and responding to the other so that the speaker has the experience, perhaps for the first time, of feeling felt by another."[3] This healing happens when the body of Christ functions as it was designed, meeting our vulnerability with loving-kindness.

But bodies don't always function like they should, do they? Ultimately, the family of God is still a broken family filled with sinful people. The body of Christ is composed of parts that are limited and still being perfected as they battle against sinful desires. And so, naturally, sometimes they hurt each other. People say the wrong thing when you're struggling. They might offer unsolicited parenting advice. They may not show up for you the way you'd hoped. This, too, is another opportunity for transformation. You see, as we experience relational rupture in the family of God, and as we respond to those hurts by practicing reconciliation—confronting one another, apologizing to one another, and forgiving one another—we experience what psychologists call earned secure attachment, or the new way of relating to the world and others as a result of healing through experiencing healthy attachment. This can rewire our brains and heal broken places in our hearts, helping us to connect more readily and in healthier ways with our kids.

Gather with Others to Worship God and Rehearse the Gospel

Apart from deep relationships, communal worship also plays a significant role in our personal transformation. Sunday mornings at church are like a weekly family reunion, reminding us of our shared bond and common mission. Paul exhorts believers in Ephesians 5:19 to speak to one another with psalms, hymns, and spiritual songs. This is what we do in Sabbath worship. The liturgy shapes us: Worship reorients our hearts, taking communion strengthens us (giving our doubting hearts something tangible to hold), hearing the Word preached challenges us, confessing our sin frees us from guilt, and receiving assurance of pardon moves our hearts to rest and rejoicing.

A pastor once recommended that, rather than bowing our heads in prayer during communion, we lift them and watch as the body of Christ walks forward to receive his provision for us. On any given Sunday, my faith is strengthened as I see people, whose stories and struggles I know, walk forward in faith and repentance.

Considering God's faithfulness in the stories and lives of these people and how he has worked through their faith, however small, and their failures, however large, helps me to see him at work in my life too.

Who Is Walking with You in Motherhood?

As a mom who longs to be self-controlled and to parent with intentionality and proactivity, you can't afford to ignore the role that community plays in your life. It can help you become less reactive by supporting your healing, holding you accountable, and reminding you of the gospel. To become the mom you long to be, you need other people to hear your story, to have eyes on your life, to love you, and to link arms with you. Sin thrives in the darkness, but community shines the kind of light on your life that helps good things grow in its place.

My friend Karen Hodge, who works tirelessly to serve and equip women's ministry leaders, regularly describes community as walking each other home. Are you known in your local church? Do you know others? If you're not rooted in community, you're missing out on key nutrients that God has prescribed for your nourishment. And your local church is missing out on being known, loved, and served by you. If you want to be the most faithful, Christlike mother possible, start by tethering yourself to the family God has given you.

Parenting Connection

As a child, I remember my mom taking us to sing to Mrs. Rose. We made sock puppets and held them up to the window of her hospital room as our portable CD player played "Let the Sunshine In." Every Christmas Eve, we would carol to people in our church who were grieving or shut-in. Every Valentine's Day, we brought flowers to a widowed friend and a stuffed animal for her daughter. We knew, always, that we were part of a family. Our church was our family.

The December when I was five, my dad's dad was in the ICU several hours away from our home. The month was spent in limbo, traditions overtaken by the back-and-forth of traveling to see him every weekend. When my parents returned from his funeral days before Christmas, they walked into a home that had been cleaned top to bottom and a Christmas tree set up in the corner of our living room by friends from church. Older couples welcomed us into their homes for Sunday lunch, standing in as surrogate grandparents for my sisters and me. Their love shaped us.

Among the top eight indicators of whether kids remain involved in church after leaving home are that they regularly served and participated in church mission activities and that they were connected with several adults in their church who were intentionally invested in them.[4] The benefits of a church community are not just for you; they're for your kids too. Don't let them miss out on being known and loved by the family of God. Don't deny them the chance to have relationships with older people. And don't let them forgo the formative experience of serving alongside you as you care for others.

Believe It for Your Motherhood

By God's design, participation in community life and the local church is essential to growing up into a more spiritually mature mom, one who is increasingly resilient, whole, compassionate, and empathetic.

Let us hold unswervingly to the hope we profess, for he who promised is faithful. And let us consider how we may spur one another on toward love and good deeds, not giving up meeting together, as some are in the habit of doing, but encouraging one another—and all the more as you see the Day approaching.
—Hebrews 10:23–25

Apply It to Your Parenting

- Take your kids with you to serve people in your church.
- Find a body of believers to worship and do life with.
- As a family, commit to gathering with other believers weekly.
- If there is a small group option for your kids, like kids' club or Sunday school, make an effort to get them there so that they too can have that additional age-specific community and instruction.

Chapter 8

Enduring Life's Difficulties (Hardship)

Once, when my kids were sick, I battled for an hour and forty-five minutes to try to get my son to take the disgusting-tasting liquid medicine. He gagged and protested. I put it into smoothies and chocolate milk. Finally, as I triumphantly administered the last of the dose, he gagged and threw up the entire contents of his stomach. The floor was covered in vomit. The dose wasted. A morning gone.

Motherhood is filled with hardship. And the range is broad.

The women in my world are doing the already challenging work of motherhood amid some *really* hard things: grieving the death of a husband, experiencing the loss of a child, suffering the sting of an extramarital affair, parenting a child who bangs his head against the wall every day, fostering high schoolers, carrying a baby who likely won't survive outside the womb, caring for aging parents, grieving the loss of a friend with terminal cancer, navigating job loss, dealing with chronic illness in themselves and illness in their kids: brain tumors, heart defects, leukemia. These are real women in my real world. I've thought about them as I crafted this section, and I've thought about you too.

I've tried to imagine what sort of suffering you've endured or might currently be walking through. I'd much rather sit with you and listen to you than talk at you . . . or type at you. But I also can't write a book about spiritual formation and motherhood without addressing the role of suffering and hardship in transformation.

There Is Purpose in Our Pain

One of the primary ways that God strengthens us, transforming us into the likeness of Christ, is through heat,[1] or hardship. For this reason, the author of James invites us to adopt an attitude of pure joy toward hardship, writing, "Consider it pure joy . . . whenever you face trials of many kinds, because you know that the testing of your faith produces perseverance. Let perseverance finish its work so that you may be mature and complete, not lacking anything" (James 1:2–4).

When it comes to difficulty, most of us are tempted to say, "Yeah, I think I'll pass." Here's the thing, though: Suffering is an inescapable reality of life in a fallen world. Did you notice that James didn't say, "*if* you face trials"—he said, "*whenever* you face trials." One of the things I love most about the Bible is how brutally honest it is about the hard realities of living in a fallen world. There's not a single day we don't wake up to the reality that things are not as they should be, and it affects us all day long, from the stomach virus ripping through our home, to the screaming of a dysregulated toddler, to the spilling of milk onto a freshly mopped floor.

And those moments are exposing. Nothing exposed how much I needed to change like the trial that is potty training. The word for "testing" that James uses in verse 3 isn't like an exam; it's the same word used to describe the purification process of precious metals during which they are boiled, bringing all the impurities to the top. That's what the heat of trial does for believers—it operates like a refiner's fire, exposing what needs to change, bringing to the surface the things we place our faith in that aren't Jesus.

The good news is that, like those precious metals, everything that the heat of hardship exposes in us, God can redeem and refine.

Suffering Clarifies Our Purpose

When facing difficulty, have you ever asked, "What's the point?" My friend Sarah is a single mom of four young kids. I was surprised recently when she referred to the demise of her marriage as one of the best things that ever happened to her. "When my husband took a two-by-four to all the dreams that I had for myself and my life, I laid there in the rubble asking what I was going to build now. Living for myself hadn't worked. I knew then that I was here for God. I wanted what he wanted for me. I was going to live for him. It was all I had to live for."

Psychologist Jonathan Haidt writes, "Trauma . . . shatters belief systems and robs people of their sense of meaning. In doing so, it forces people to put the pieces back together, and often they do so by [turning to] God . . . as a unifying principle."[2] Hardship exposes the agenda we have for our life and often thwarts it in such a powerful a way that we're left looking for a new one. Trials force us out of the pattern of living for ourselves and free us to live for God.

The first question of the Westminster Shorter Catechism

declares that the chief end of man is to glorify God and enjoy him forever.[3] We can therefore conclude that the entire point of our lives and existence, and consequently our motherhood, is to bring glory to God and enjoy him. This pursuit is what will bring us the greatest satisfaction. In his book *Walking with God Through Pain and Suffering*, Tim Keller, summarizing several assertions of C. S. Lewis, writes, "God commands us to glorify him because it is only by doing this that we will ever find the rest, satisfaction, and joy in him that we were made for."[4] Suffering often serves to clarify this purpose. Hardship removes our hope from created things or our own goals and aspirations and invites us to consider God's priority list, and God himself, as the source of satisfaction and purpose. No earthly source of satisfaction can compare to the surpassing weight of fellowship with Jesus (Philippians 3:7–9).

Any discontentment and disillusionment we experience in motherhood invites us to remove our hope for fulfillment from any vocation (being a mom), person (our kids), or experience (motherhood) and invites us to place it instead in God himself. You were made for glory. You were made to reflect God's glory (his beauty, love, and holiness) and to enjoy God's glory (to find your deepest satisfaction and identity in him). The problem is, rather than looking for the glory we were designed for from our designer, we seek that feeling of purpose, affirmation, and worth from other places, and sometimes even motherhood.[5] That's why difficulty in motherhood can be so clarifying. Any dissatisfaction we feel with our experience of motherhood invites us to move from trying to get glory from our kids or our role as their mom to trying to *give* glory to God with our motherhood. And as we give him glory, we receive from him the glory we were made for—we become more of who we were created to be and experience more satisfaction in him. And this bears the fruit of the Spirit in our lives, making us the mothers—the people—we long to be.

But we easily forget this, don't we? Though our spiritual shoulders seem easily shaken by realities like death and tragedy, jostling us awake, we often fail to see the purpose in lesser trials, like stubbing our toes, sitting in traffic, staying up all night with a screaming baby, or struggling to shepherd a child through a meltdown. But James calls us to recognize the benefit of trials of "many kinds," not just those of the extreme variety, since as believers, this is how we develop perseverance, becoming mature and complete (James 1:2). Righteousness and peace—those are his intended purposes for us within hardship, along with character, endurance, and hope (Hebrews 12:11; Romans 5:3–5).

Suffering Builds Our Dependence on God

A friend of mine recently mentioned that she felt like God had used her experience of infertility to make her a better mom. I expected her to say she was more grateful for her kids because of the hardship she endured to have them, but instead she said that the painful waiting and the experience of God's comfort in suffering had made her a more patient, empathetic, and compassionate mom. I found the same to be true in pregnancy loss and hard seasons in my marriage. The maturation of character that comes from intimacy with and dependence on God overflows into how we shepherd and care for our children.

In no way am I trying to deny that suffering is painful. From a colicky baby to an unfaithful spouse, life can hurt. God's goal is not to turn us into stoics who experience hardship without tears or into people who are unaffected by suffering. And he's not trying to turn us into people who *like* suffering. But he invites us to turn to him and to depend on him for comfort, strength, support, and the power to endure.

You can cathartically cry out to God, "This doesn't feel good," or "This feels like too much." And as you do, remember that he is with you, comforting and strengthening you by his Spirit. Remember, change is relational, so the more dependent we are on God, the more reliant we are on fellowship with him, the closer we are to him, the more like him we will be.

Endure Hardship as a Loved Child

The writer of Hebrews instructs believers to "endure hardship as discipline" (12:7), adding that God disciplines those he *loves* for their good so they may share in his holiness (v. 10). The word translated "discipline" doesn't mean punishment—it's not a spanking, it's a shaping. Like James, the author of Hebrews doesn't discriminate as to what kind of trial. It's not as if some trials have the potential to transform us and others don't. As believers, we can endure all our hardships as purposeful, because they are training us to be holy. In this way, hardship helps to make holiness our concern. And when holiness is our concern, not comfort or self-preservation, it changes how we experience difficulty, especially in motherhood.

It's said, or rather sung if you're Kelly Clarkson, that what doesn't kill you makes you stronger, but that's not necessarily true. Two people can endure the same trial but be affected in entirely different ways. So what makes the difference? It's the posture we take in the face of hardship. Think of it this way: When I do a dead lift, if I want it to make me stronger, I focus on engaging certain muscle groups to lift with good form. But if I bear the weight with no thought of purpose, the likelihood of injury is high. Understanding God's purposes for us in suffering is what causes it to have its intended effect.

But we also need to remember God's *heart* toward us. Maybe your suffering has caused you to become suspicious that God doesn't care or isn't loving. Maybe you feel like instead of God putting you in the refiner's fire, he has forgotten you and left you in the kiln.

At a recent retreat, I met a woman who told me that during the dark days of her five-year-old's unexplained seizures, she was so thankful that God's goodness, wisdom, and love for her as his child were already settled in her soul. That way, she didn't have to fight a "double battle." She faced the trial rooted in the reality that God loved her, and even as she lamented and begged for a new season, she was able to endure the one she was in. God's spirit assures us that we are children of God—that we are loved daughters—as we undergo this discipline of hardship (Romans 8:16).

As mortal moms with limited knowledge and attention, we don't always know or do what's best for our kids. But God is a perfectly wise parent who always disciplines us for our good. The writer of Hebrews alludes to this, saying that our parents "disciplined us for a little while as they thought best; but God disciplines us for our good, in order that we may share in his holiness" (Hebrews 12:10).

"He knows what is best for each one of us. He doesn't have to debate with Himself over what is most suitable for us. He knows intuitively and perfectly the nature, intensity, and duration of adversity that will best serve His purpose to make us partakers of His holiness."[6]

This doesn't mean your suffering is justified. The world is unjust. And we won't always know all the reasons for our pain, but we can know within those trials that God loves us, that he is committed to our good, and that he won't waste an ounce of the hardship we experience.

Keep Your Eyes on the Prize

As you face difficulties in motherhood, don't lose heart. You might feel like you're wasting away, but you're being inwardly renewed. However heavy or unending your troubles may feel, they are preparing you for eternal glory that will make them seem light and momentary by comparison (2 Corinthians 4:16–18).

You can look to God in the challenges you face, knowing he is using them to transform you into the mom he created you to be, a mom who bears fruit and looks like Jesus and loves what he loves. I've heard Joni Eareckson Tada say on more than one occasion that God will use what he hates to accomplish what he loves. As you face hardship, remember, God loves you too much to leave you where you are.

Think of the last hard thing you experienced, big or small. How did you respond? What might it have looked like to "endure it as discipline"? Today, each time you experience difficulty, whether you're sitting in traffic with a screaming baby or meeting the resistance of a child, try praying this prayer:

> Father, I know that you love me and are with me. Please fix my eyes on you and help me endure [name the particular difficulty] as discipline. Please use this hardship to make me more like Jesus.

Parenting Connection

We must be careful that we don't rob our children of the opportunity to be shaped by hardship. Our love for our kids often leads us to want to shelter them from pain and difficulty, but shielding kids from hard things can hinder their growth and prevent them from developing essential skills to navigate life with resilience and flexibility as adults.[7] For them to grow, we need to allow our kids to take risks and experience challenges. We can help them to see the problems they face as an opportunity for growth and transformation. Often when we're waiting for something, I'll say to my kids, "This is an opportunity for us to grow our patience muscles! Let's ask the Holy Spirit to use this waiting experience to train us." Lord willing, when they're older, they'll see adversity as an opportunity for the maturation of Christian character.

Similarly, sometimes my fear of "messing up" my kids or my guilt over ways that I have failed them, or even my desire for things to be easy, prevents me from holding boundaries that might feel uncomfortable for them or even allowing my kids to experience, rather than rescuing them from, the natural consequences of their actions. The book of Proverbs says that a parent who loves their child disciplines them with diligence and care (Proverbs 13:24). Don't be afraid of setting limits and holding to them. However uncomfortable your child's pushback may feel, this is loving. And don't be afraid to let them experience the consequences of irresponsibility or disobedience. Going hungry or getting a zero for forgotten homework might better serve them than you delivering their forgotten lunch or homework, even if you fear they'll be upset with you or accuse you of being unloving. Just as God disciplines those he loves, we ought to discipline our children. If you lack wisdom as to how to guide them, pray and ask God, who gives it generously (James 1:5).

Believe It for Your Motherhood

God matures his children through the hardships they face. So rather than running from pain and difficulty, you can endure it knowing that it, like a refining fire, can transform you into a more Christlike mom.

Not only so, but we also glory in our sufferings, because we know that suffering produces perseverance; perseverance, character; and character, hope. And hope does not put us to shame, because God's love has been poured out into our hearts through the Holy Spirit, who has been given to us.

—Romans 5:3–5

Apply It to Your Parenting

- Instead of trying to keep your kids from experiencing difficulty or shielding them from pain, help them learn to see it as an opportunity for growth.
- Acknowledge the difficulties you and your children face. Then use the phrase "This is an opportunity to grow in ____ [insert fruit of the Spirit]."
- Don't be afraid to set boundaries and let your kids experience natural consequences.

Part 3

Parenting Well as a Work in Progress

Chapter 9

Embracing the Process

"Can we skip to the good part?"[1]

These lyrics from the band AJR have lived rent-free in my brain since the social media trend in which the snap of a finger instantly transformed a muddy yard to a newly sodded one, a cluttered pantry to a color-coded organizational masterpiece, or unstyled hair into an updo.

Who doesn't love a good before-and-after? What resonates about this trend is the desire to skip the part *between* before and after. We love a good transformation, but we hate the process of being transformed.

It's not all that surprising, really. Our culture doesn't exactly give us a ton of practice with patience, as AI answers our questions in seconds and Amazon Prime delivers anything we could possibly need in just two days. We're not accustomed to waiting. Why should we be surprised when that same impatience shows up in our approach to personal change in motherhood?

But that impatience isn't just about us; it shows up because we love our kids. We want to snap our fingers and be different so that we can stop negatively affecting them. We want to show up to the task of motherhood as a psychologically healthy, emotionally available, and spiritually mature mom. And we want it now.

Here's the thing, though: Scripture—and nature, for that matter—would suggest that God *loves* the transformation process. Apparently, it's his favorite way to work. We see this in the way he created the world. He didn't snap his finger to turn "without form and void" (Genesis 1:2 ESV) into lush and fully populated. Sure, he spoke the world into being, but he did it over the span of six days, and even then, it was a world at the beginning of what it would become—a world in process.

God welcomed Adam and Eve to participate in this process, asking them to help grow the garden and to fill it with people through childbirth. We see God's preference for process in the way that redemptive history unfolds, including his leading the Israelites in the desert for forty years instead of simply teleporting them to the promised land. We see it in his continued created order in nature. A seed falls to the ground, it germinates, it pokes up through the dirt, and slowly it grows until it buds and flowers. Even Jesus grew in wisdom and in stature (Luke 2:52). God works in process. Creation and redemptive history reveal that it's his preferred method of operation. The same is true in the sanctification of his people. Should we expect anything different for the way that he matures moms?

Understanding the stages of God's change process helps us to stop striving for perfection in parenting. Justification—being declared righteous because of the finished work of Jesus—frees us from the need to be seen as perfect, to measure up, or to use motherhood to gain approval. Jesus was perfect for us, and we are fully accepted in him. Sanctification—the ongoing work of the Spirit through which we are made more like Christ—helps us to embrace change as a process, seeing ourselves humbly and graciously as works in progress instead of resenting our *lack* of progress. And glorification—the future hope we have of being free from sin—frees us from the expectation that perfection is even possible on this side of heaven, helping us run with endurance, knowing with confident hope that one day we will be perfected.

Letting Go of Perfection

Recently, I was telling someone about the effect that researching for and writing this book have had on my life. Being saturated in this content has made such a difference in my parenting. "I don't even remember the last time I yelled at my kids!" I told them. Welp, I couldn't say that the next day. And I didn't just yell at them; I turned from yelling at them and sort of just yelled into the middle of the room, like a crazy person screaming into a pillow, except there was no pillow.

When I stopped yelling (both *at* them and into the middle of the room), got my kids and myself in the car, and finally backed out of the driveway (of course we were rushing to get somewhere #onbrand), the feeling I had reminded me of the board game Can't Stop, where you make so much progress only to lose it all in one roll. Negative self-thoughts poured in. Truly, I thought I was past this struggle and on to another one, a more manageable one, a less obvious one, a less traumatizing one. Nope. As it turns out, I'm still a mom who yells.

When was the last time you felt like the house of cards fell? When was the last time your sin reared its ugly head, and the exposure led you to lament your lack of progress? How did you respond to that feeling of failure?

In his article "Perfectionism Will Only Make You Miserable," professor of practical theology Jeremy Pierre defines perfectionism as "the tendency to expect flawless performance from self and others, resulting in frustration at any sign of failure."[2] He says that a perfectionist is unwilling to accept two truths that God says about all people: one, that we're all limited as human beings and, two, that we are all fallen sinners. "In the end," he writes, "perfectionism is the ongoing attempt to need Jesus less."[3] That hits hard for me. I often find that I want Jesus to fix me more than I want Jesus himself. I don't want to need him. But as we've established, the goal of the Christian life, and therefore your life as a Christian mom, is dependence.

Perfect parenting is the enemy of faithful (or faith-filled) parenting because when we are trying to need God less, we cannot possibly depend on him more. And depending on him is the only way we can be the moms he created us to be.

Letting Go of the Need to Perform or Prove Yourself in Motherhood

I am always hyperaware of my kids' behavior when we're at family gatherings. There is no shortage of opinions, glances, and cryptic comments. I want my kids to act a certain way, and I want to respond to them a certain way, so that I'll be perceived as a good mom. But the irony is, I end up being a terrible version of me when I am focused on how people perceive me. The poor behavior of my kids feels like a nuclear threat, and my poor reaction is almost guaranteed by how high the stakes feel. I imagine their thoughts: "Look at her, she's giving parenting advice to people on the internet, and she can't even put her kids to bed without a major meltdown."

But I don't feel this way just around family; I also crave the approval of women in my church and even my peers. Sometimes I even fear the opinions of the imagined adult versions of my children, not wanting them to blame or resent me.

Just think about your last public interaction with your kid, maybe at the grocery store or at church. Do you know the feeling of being more upset with someone witnessing a negative interaction than about how that interaction affected your child? The problem here is that a fear of others' opinions leads us to be more concerned with *looking* like a bad mom than with what is going on in our hearts—which, ironically, leads us to act in a way that *is* wrong. True, lasting, biblical change requires that we focus not on the approval we desire from others but on the approval we already have from our loving heavenly Father. It requires that we align our concern with his rather than being ruled by the opinions of people.

"You are a good mom." I long to hear these words, don't you? The benediction that you and I crave is spoken over us at salvation because the perfect life of Christ and his atoning work are applied to us. "Good" is not an accolade you have to work for; it's a verdict you've received. And that verdict is delivered by the judge of all the earth, who is indeed the most qualified to judge, the one whose opinion matters more than any other opinion.

Letting Go of the Need to Measure Up

Some time ago, my literary agent sent me a little book called *There Are Moms Way Worse Than You: Irrefutable Proof That You Are Indeed a Fantastic Parent*.[4] The book, which is hilarious and admittedly relieving, details the bizarre habits of animal mothers to provide comfort for moms who feel like failures. For example, don't feel bad about having a dirty house; beetles raise their kids in decomposing animals.

Though we often employ comparison to try to make ourselves feel better, it ultimately leads to discouragement. In my less shiny moments, I have often soothed myself with the knowledge that I'm doing a lot better than the average mom. But sometimes, in my not-so-great moments, I think about the moms who look like they have it all together. Comparison and envy pop up all over Scripture, and every time, they distract people from the purpose of God for their lives and move them to act out of a sinful desire. Joseph's brothers sell him into slavery, David kills Uriah, Sarai abuses Hagar, Rachel resents Leah and fails to love Jacob well. *If we aren't careful, looking around instead of up can cause us to worship and pursue an idealized version of motherhood instead of Jesus himself.* But the ideal version of motherhood is the most Christlike version of you.

Pay attention to when you feel envy, pride, or discouragement. If you are filled with envy, ask God to help you to be the most Christlike version of you, with *your* personality, for *your* kids, and in *your* particular circumstances. If you feel pride, intercede for the mom who is struggling. In humility, you can thank God for his work in your life, acknowledging that any good comes from Jesus. If you feel discouraged, let that lead you to seek comfort from God's Word. It could be that the discouragement you feel is actually godly sorrow over sinful failure. If God is using the Christlike example of another mom to convict you of sin, confess according to his Word, receive the relief of his pardon, and ask not to be more like *her* but to be more like *Christ.*

When we compare ourselves to others to feel "good enough," we lose sight of our unique capacity, weaknesses, and calling. When we make another mom the standard for what it means to be a "good mom," we take our eyes off Jesus, who is not just a perfect example but a perfect Savior who provides the grace we need to grow and change.

Trusting Jesus to be our perfect Savior, the one who frees us from the pressure to perform and the need to be perfect, also takes that burden off our children. When we know that Jesus has given us his perfect record, we don't have to treat our kids' behavior as the test by which our character or efforts in motherhood will be graded.

Persevering Beyond Perceived Lack of Progress

Imagine a set of stairs with no railings on either side, with a large rectangular trampoline beside it. This is the set of French dancer and choreographer Yoann Bourgeois's "Staircase" routine. In this performance, Yoann begins at the bottom step and ascends a few stairs, getting closer and closer to the edge with every step until he falls off the edge of the staircase. He lands on the trampoline, springing him back up into the air. The wonder of the routine is that he lands perfectly upright on the step he just fell off of and then continues to climb. Over and over, he climbs a little higher, falls off the staircase to the left, and springs back up onto the steps.[5]

Each time Yoann falls off the staircase, it appears as if he's lost all the ground that he gained. Isn't this how we feel when we see our sin? We fall, and it seems as if we've made no progress at all, as if we've lost all the ground we had gained. "I thought I had risen above this," we may think. But what if we thought of God's grace like the trampoline in Yoann's routine? The farther up the staircase Yoann is when he falls, the deeper he descends into the trampoline. The deeper he goes into that trampoline, the more those springs stretch and the higher he springs, right back to where he was before.

Sometimes, though, after failure, we feel not just that we're back where we started but that we're actually worse than ever. Here's why: The closer we get to God, the holier he seems to us, and the holier he seems to us, the more aware we will be of the ways we aren't like him in comparison. This means that the process of becoming a more holy mom can feel like we're becoming a *less* holy mom. But here's the thing: Our view of grace grows right along with our awareness of sin. The more serious our sin appears to us, the deeper into the trampoline of grace we will go, and the deeper we go into that grace, the higher we will spring into joy. And our joy and dependence grow, propelling us to take the next step on the journey to becoming like Jesus.

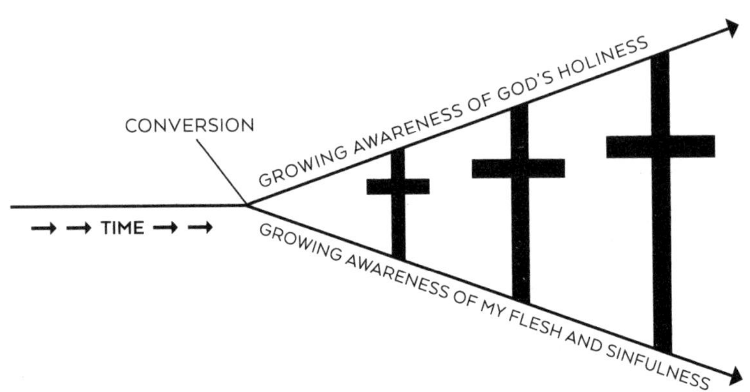

Arrow Chart

The more you grow in the knowledge of God's holiness, the worse your sin will seem. But the bigger the gap between your sinfulness and God's holiness appears, the greater your view of grace will become. And the greater your view of grace, the more like Jesus you'll become.[6]

A friend of mine recently told me that when her shortcomings are exposed, she is tempted to check out, to return to old patterns from before she became a Christian—seeking escape from conviction, a break from striving, and relief from feeling bad about herself. Yoann's routine would be pretty different if he fell to the right instead of the left—onto the floor instead of the trampoline. I imagine rather than continuing to climb, hitting the hard ground would lead him to quit the routine. But we do this very thing in the Christian life. Instead of running to God when we fail, we don't run to grace but instead toss our hands up and give in to what I call "whatever" behavior. Or as Jackie Hill Perry puts it, we return to our own vomit because our appetites aren't changing fast enough.[7] It's the spiritual equivalent of dumping out a whole pitcher just because you spilled a few drops.

Remember, the grace that saved you is the same grace that changes you. So every time you fail, rather than giving in to frustration or self-loathing, reach for gospel gratitude. Let go of your perceived lack of progress, and instead let all your imperfections plunge you into grace and spring you up into the joy that fuels obedience.

Whatever need it may expose, when you become aware of the ways that you don't look like Jesus or fall short of biblical mandates, you can praise God for his sufficiency. Those moments reveal what we already know: There's still a need for transformation, and the good news is, God is committed enough to your transformation to reveal that to you.

I so desperately want to "arrive" in motherhood, to reach the point where I handle everything exactly how I hope to, where I always know exactly what to do, and where I respond with wisdom and never blow it. Time and time again, I respond to my own shortcomings with shock and disbelief. But our ongoing struggle with sin in motherhood does not surprise God. He's not shocked that you and I aren't farther along. And you don't need to be either.

Seeing and Celebrating Change

While it is good to be aware of what needs to change, one danger of being focused on our failures or preoccupied with our lack of progress is that we cannot recognize and celebrate the ways we are changing! The truth is, God is transforming us, from one degree of glory to another, into moms who look more and more like Jesus.

Just yesterday, I excused myself and walked out the door during a heated moment with my boys. It was loud; I was overstimulated and, honestly, just angry. "I love you boys," I told my kids. "I'm going to step away for a minute and talk to Jesus so I don't talk to you in a way that I'll regret."

As I walked outside, I berated myself for lacking self-control, for being easily angered, for not being more at peace in moments like that. But then the Holy Spirit moved my heart to praise as I realized he *was* bearing the fruit of self-control in my life, evidenced by the decision to walk outside. I was frustrated with myself for being angry, but I realized I had been obedient to the biblical mandate, "In your anger do not sin" (Ephesians 4:26).

I almost missed it! I almost missed the opportunity to rejoice. And I don't want that to happen to you. You're changing, for Christ's sake! And that's not taking his name in vain, by the way! By God, you're changing! You're a work-in-progress mom. And we're going to celebrate!

Celebration is an important tool on the road to change because it puts us in a position not only to petition God for his help but also to praise him for it. He's worthy of that. And also, that praise propels us forward as it protects us from the discouragement that comes with preoccupation with shortcomings. By design, the Christian life is a lifelong commitment to growth and change. And God has promised to bring that growth and change to completion (Philippians 1:6). Knowing that that day is coming, having faith in his promise, helps us to persevere through failure because we know we're being perfected.

Celebration might feel like pride to you, but it doesn't have to sound like, "I'm so proud of me!" It can sound like, "I'm grateful for God's enabling grace." My boys and I recently took a day trip to a zoo about two-and-a-half hours away. Among other setbacks, there was limited parking, and it rained, but we had a fabulous time. I reflected on a previous zoo trip and what it had felt like for me—riddled with anxiety and discontent. There had been shouting and tears. The contrast was remarkable. The growth was undeniable.

When we got in the car, my boys and I had a little dance party celebration for God's kindness in giving us such an enjoyable time despite challenging circumstances. "I was exactly the mom I wanted to be today," I wrote in my journal that night. "Thank you, God, for your enabling grace!"

This journal entry served as a little Ebenezer, a reminder of God's faithfulness, like the pile of rocks by the Jordan River after it parted.[8] It was a reminder of God's help. I walked into the next day encouraged and expectant, with eyes more committed to seeing evidence of God's work in my heart and life.

Can you make a little rock pile today? Find ways that God is answering your prayers, providing for you, or bearing fruit in your mothering, and make a list of these, stacking them like stones of remembrance. You might even enlist your kids in helping you notice these. Teach them the fruits of the Spirit (so many songs for this!) and ask them to watch for God producing them in your life. Maybe keep a note on your phone of ways God helped you, moments you showed up as you hoped, and times you resisted temptation. It's important to be on guard against our sin, but it's also important to celebrate change. Commit to looking for and being willing to recognize God's faithfulness, and praise him when you see the fruit his Spirit bears in your life.

Fruit doesn't grow quickly. You can't rush it. But you can faithfully be on the lookout for it. And as you expectantly watch for it, you can enjoy the process. Each bud, each flower, is thrilling if you have the right perspective. You might be a work in progress, but what you are becoming is truly incredible. Enjoy the journey.

Parenting Connection

It's easy to recognize areas where our kids need to grow, but are we as quick to see what they're doing well? One phrase that helps me with this is saying, "I see God at work in you!" I learned this phrase working for a college ministry. "Growth in grace" was a goal of the ministry, and so we celebrated and highlighted God's work in the girls we were working with. I love using this phrase with my kids for two reasons: First, it gives glory and honor to God for any good thing. He's worthy of that! And second, it helps prevent the kids from feeling like everything depends on them and developing a white-knuckle approach to their sanctification. This protects them from both pride and discouragement. It also inherently reminds our kids that they are people still in process.

And if you're wondering if you have to know if your kids are regenerate before saying something like this to them, remember, any good comes from God, whether it's saving grace, enabling grace for his children, or common grace for humanity. So I am fully comfortable saying to all my kids, "You chose kindness! I see God at work in you!" Or when I snuggle them at night, "I noticed today how you considered others more important than yourself. I see God at work in you." This also protects *my* heart, reminding me that I can plant and water, but it's God who gives the growth.

In certain seasons, I've printed out charts of the fruit of the Spirit and let my kids add stars to the charts when they display godly character. This trains my eyes to see the good work God is doing, and it helps them to see it too!

It's also important for us to remember that our kids are still learning and growing in a physical and cognitive way. We can love them by meeting them where they are developmentally. This means, for one, making sure that our expectations of them are developmentally appropriate. For example, not burdening your toddler with four-step commands (go shower, brush your teeth, clear your floor, and . . .) when they can only process and remember two. Sure, we can help our kids grow and seek to equip them with the ability to sit still for longer periods of time, or follow through with a task, or regulate their emotions, but we can also let them be children, making an effort to understand what's happening in their brains and bodies at any given age as they grow according to God's design.

Your response to the failure of your children (and to your own) will help shape their response to their failures. Find a trampoline to jump on and talk about repentance. Train them to run to grace and spring back up into joy. Pray with them when they're feeling guilty or discouraged. When your kids are tough on themselves, you might encourage them with this refrain I like to use with my boys:

You're a person in process,
still learning and growing.
God is working in you!
Don't give up, keep going!

Believe It for Your Motherhood

God has already declared you righteous because of the finished work of Jesus, so you don't have to worry about the opinions of others or how you measure up as a mom. And his design for Christian maturation is a process, so you don't have to resent your lack of perfection. Instead, commit to responding to your failure by falling into grace, and let gospel gratitude and joy fuel your obedience. Celebrate the ways that you see God at work. He's committed to completing the work he began in you!

He who began a good work in you will carry it on to completion until the day of Christ Jesus.
—Philippians 1:6

Apply It to Your Parenting

- Memorize the fruits of the Spirit with your kids and point them out in each other's lives.
- Consider making a sticker chart for when you see the fruit of

the Spirit displayed in one another. Put yourself on the chart too!

- When you see growth or maturity in your kids, celebrate by saying, "I see God at work in you!"
- When your kids are tough on themselves, encourage them with this refrain:

You're a person in process,
still learning and growing.
God is working in you!
Don't give up, keep going!

- Find a trampoline and talk to your kids about letting failure plunge them into God's grace and spring them back up into joy-fueled obedience.

Chapter 10

Practicing Repair

Remember the story where I slammed on the brakes, the puppy crashed into the dashboard, and my scared kids sobbed after I shamed them? Psychologists would call that event a "rupture." Left unrepaired, a rupture leads to "a deepening sense of disconnection between parent and child." And prolonged disconnection can create "shame and humiliation that is toxic for a child's growing sense of self."[1]

If your concern is, as the title of this book suggests, not messing up your kids, then research suggests that you've got to learn to repair these ruptures. The Bible also describes repairing broken relationships as a key element of the Christian life.

God's Word places a high value on humility and repentance, encouraging believers to own their mistakes and confess their sins to one another (James 5:16). Paul instructs the members of the church at Rome to be at peace with one another, as far as it depends on them, implying that where rupture occurs, it should be followed by an effort to restore relationship (Romans 12:18). In Matthew

18:15–17, Jesus urges his followers to address conflict directly as a first step of reconciliation. He also tells them that if they are offering a gift at the altar, and there remember that someone has something against them, they are to leave their gift and go and be reconciled to them and then come back and offer their gift (Matthew 5:23–24). This applies to us as parents when we have wronged our kids.

So how do we walk in accordance with these mandates from Scripture as we seek to be at peace with and protect the development of our littlest neighbors?

Let's use my puppy-dashboard-shame-speech event as a little guinea pig, shall we? We'll just pick up where we left off, with my kids all in their rooms for quiet time and me having a good cry on my bed.

Recognize the Rupture

Ruptures can be relatively minor, and they don't always occur because Mom loses her cool. Sometimes they are simply the friction that comes with a parent setting a loving limit that a kid isn't a fan of. As my middle child often tells me, limits don't *feel* loving at all. So in that case, the need for repair is simply that the child needs to be reminded that they are loved despite the feeling they have when their mom doesn't give them what they want.

Sometimes ruptures aren't the result of our fallen human condition so much as our limited human capacity. Ruptures can happen when we simply *misattune* to the emotions of our children. For example, a rupture might occur if I joke about something my son doesn't think is funny. When I notice the tears in his eyes or the heat in his cheeks, I can initiate repair by saying, "Hey, buddy, your face is telling me that you didn't think that was funny. I'm sorry I joked in a way that hurt you." It is important to remember that friction doesn't always mean you are wrong or that you have sinned against your kids. Repent of what needs to be repented of, and reconcile after unintentional hurts. But don't feel guilty about holding boundaries (that's loving) or having misunderstandings (that's human).

The sort of rupture that occurred in *this* story, however, is called a "toxic rupture." A "toxic rupture" occurs when an incident involves "intense emotional distress and a despairing disconnection between a parent and child."[2] The reason these ruptures are considered toxic is because they result in an "intense feeling of overwhelming shame."[3] After something like this happens, kids often experience a physiological reaction, like a tummy ache, an impulse to run and hide, a headache, or a tight chest.

When my young kids were in their rooms for quiet time after the rupture, they experienced shame and were trying to make sense of what just happened. Because young children tend to see themselves as the center of their little worlds, they often also believe that they are responsible for their caregiver's actions and emotions. So after a toxic rupture, rather than thinking that Mommy is mean, a child is more likely to think of themselves as bad or defective for making Mommy upset. Blaming themselves can serve as a coping mechanism that helps kids feel less powerless over their circumstances.[4]

Now, even when my kids' behavior is wrong or needs correction, even though they are sinful and need saving, they also have inherent dignity because they are made in the image of God. And the fact of the matter is my kids are never responsible for *my* actions.

Although my kids' behavior presented an occasion for my sin to show up, their behavior did not *cause* my reaction. As the person responsible for guiding them into maturity, I need to own my reaction, which had little to do with *them* and much more to do with *me*. That is vital for them to understand if they are to develop into healthy adults.

Take Time for Reflection

It is imperative that repairs be timely, but it is also important that we do not attempt to repair with our children prematurely. If we engage with them when our prefrontal cortex is not back online, even if our goal is to reattune and fix the relationship, we can quickly go right back into defensiveness and shaming speech. And so it's essential for you, as the mom, to take a moment to *reflect* on what just happened.

As you reflect, ask these questions:

First, what were *you* experiencing?
Second, what was your *child* experiencing?

When you ask these two questions, you're practicing "attunement," which basically just means you're paying attention to feelings and experience.

A lack of attunement to myself is what allowed me to reach the point of slamming on the brakes and shouting. I ignored approximately one million cues leading up to the moment that I lost it. Remember that tight jaw? A lack of attunement to my kids is what made it possible to berate and shame them. I closed off from any feelings of empathy for them as little people and barreled right over them with a shame-speech bulldozer, as if they were threats or enemies, ignoring what was happening on their faces as I did it.

What does it look like to reattune to myself and to them after a toxic rupture? Think back on the categories and frameworks we've established in this book: Reflecting on these helps us move from reaction to responsibility.

1. Embrace Human Limitations

Leading up to this rupture, in what way might I have failed to live within my limits? You may recall that my stomach was grumbling. I was hungry . . . well, hangry. I was also sleep-deprived. That precious puppy needed to go potty every two hours the night before and had cried to be snuggled . . . a lot. When I planned our activities for that morning, I failed to account for the weakness and vulnerability that fatigue can bring.

2. Acknowledge the Human Condition

How did being housed in a fallen body contribute to what happened? There are two sides to this coin, remember? First, let's consider my fallen flesh. What was I loving that wasn't God or neighbor? This is painfully obvious to me. When I am not in control of my kids, it sets off all kinds of terrible inner talk. *You can't even control your own kids; what business do you have talking about parenting on the internet?* When I become dysregulated, I panic about what my inability to cope means about me. *You're so undisciplined. How can you still have so little control over your emotions after so much counseling?* As the noise level of my kids increases, my anxiety increases, and then I resent my kids more and more because I hate the way my body is responding. I also love peace and feel threatened by chaos, which is why in that moment, I was willing to sin to get it.

3. Look Beneath the Surface

Now let's turn the coin over and just think about the fact that my body doesn't function as it was designed. I have a fallen parasympathetic nervous system—it thinks I'm in danger when I'm not. My body was trying to alert me that it needed care and soothing, but I didn't punch in the alarm code or employ my resources. I ignored those cues because I didn't want to be weak. I want my anxiety symptoms to be a thing of the past. But ignoring them hardly made them go away. They just came out sideways.

4. Consider the Impact of Suffering

Finally, how did my experience as a sufferer contribute to this moment? What did my emotional baggage have to do with what happened? This event activated a particular theme in my life history: feeling ignored and helpless. Growing up, my two older sisters would often say, "I. H.," when I was trying to talk to them. They would say this and then act like I didn't exist. Years later, I learned that this was their code for "ignore her." Now, my sisters are some of my dearest friends today, but that doesn't change the fact that elementary-aged Abbey processed this as a repeatedly experienced little-*t* trauma. In those moments when it felt as if no sound was coming out of my mouth, when I honestly wondered if I had actually been muted or become invisible, I would panic, trying to figure out what to do to make them hear me.

Even as an adult, I have felt helpless like that several times in my life. I am more prone to feeling that way because those neurons that wired together still fire together when I don't feel like I have the support or the resources I need. This causes me to be keenly aware of, and often panicked by, the feeling that I am alone or without help. As I thought about this, sitting on my bed, I talked to God about the pain and asked him to heal the hurt and renew my mind, making new pathways and new connections in my brain. In that moment, I felt seen and heard by a God who loves me and listens to me.

Take Ownership Instead of Placing Blame

Taking the time to process an event allows us to take ownership of our actions instead of blaming our kids. We are then able to think of them as image bearers rather than instigators. Once I stopped *blaming* them, I was able to truly *see* them. Now that I had attuned to myself and rested in God's attunement to, forgiveness for, and acceptance of me, I could attune to them.

What were *they* feeling in the car? They felt frustrated with one another. They probably felt anxious because of the growing tension my mood created. They may have been overstimulated from watching the DVD. We were late for lunch, so they were probably all hungry. The youngest was due for a nap. They needed food, rest, support to regulate their own emotions, and assistance with conflict resolution. Instead, they got scary mommy.

I thought back on what their sweet, small faces looked like when I raised my voice. What might it have felt like to hear those words spoken to me by someone I considered a safe person? How might I feel if my husband had lowered his eyebrows and said anything beginning with "Why can't you just . . . ?" I recalled how helpless I felt when a teacher yelled at me. Knowing this feeling made my eyes fill with tears of compassion for my precious boys. My heart was filled with sorrow over the way I had hurt them.

Practice Repentance

Having considered how I had affected my littlest neighbors and having answered the question of what I had placed on the throne of my heart instead of God, I now confessed the ways that I had broken his two greatest commandments. This included acknowledging how I had lived beyond my limits, loved comfort and ease, sought to preserve my pride, and acted out of my woundedness.

After this confession, I thanked God for his forgiveness of me in Christ Jesus, for his compassion, and for the healing work he is doing within me. I asked him to free me from guilt and self-condemnation. I fell into grace and then sprang back up into joy and relief.

Then I concluded my time alone with words from Psalm 139, inviting God to search me and asking him to lead me in "the way everlasting" (v. 24)—the way that leads to life. I asked him to help me be aware of my limits, to increase my self-control, and to deliver me from the love of comfort and ease.

Then, and only then, after owning my sin before God, confessing it to him, and being assured of his love for me in Christ Jesus, did I stand up to go and talk to my kids individually to initiate repair.

Initiate Repair

Now, if I had not just spent time with the Lord, confessing my sin as mine and remembering his love for me and his acceptance of me, my apology to my kids might have sounded something like this: "I'm sorry that I yelled at you, but you guys were totally disrespectful and out of control."

Survey says: Errnnnnnnnk. (That's a buzzer sound if you needed a clue.) Not an apology.

"I'm sorry I yelled at you, but I was running on so little sleep because Annie [the puppy] kept me up all night."

Survey says: Errnnnnnnnk. Not an apology.

Both of those faux apologies excuse my behavior by blaming my kids or my circumstances. But I don't have to do that. Because I'm forgiven. I'm justified. And I am beloved. So I can call my behavior what it is. Here's what repair actually sounds like:

"Hey, I am really sorry I spoke to you the way I did. I can imagine it probably felt pretty scary to see Mom out of control like that. And I know that if someone had spoken to me like that, my feelings would have been hurt. I came in here to ask for your forgiveness and also to make sure that you know that my yelling is *not* your fault. Sure, you guys were out of control, but I could have responded with self-control. I could have managed our time better, and I could have used the tools I have to calm down. I hate that I hurt you. Will you please forgive me?"

Sometimes repair is a big conversation, like this one, but it can also be playful in subtler, nontoxic ruptures. I've often heard mom friends mention that they wish there were a redo button. And the good news is that often, in the moments we most wish we could press it, we can!

If I raise my voice or rush my kids, I often pretend to hold a remote and say, "Pause," freezing dramatically and saying, "That is *definitely* not how I want to talk to y'all." Then I can exaggerate pressing a rewind button, making the record scratch sound, or maybe even spinning in a circle and use kind, calm words like I'm always urging them to. "Whew, that's better!" The important thing is that they see me owning my mistakes when I blow it.

When They Don't Say "I Forgive You"

Best case scenario, when we genuinely ask for forgiveness from our kids, they'll offer it to us. But on the occasions when they don't, or when we find that it's hard to forgive ourselves, here's what we need to remember: God is the most qualified judge, and he offers his forgiveness to us every single time we fail. Knowing this—believing this—protects our children from bearing the burden of providing us absolution.

In the long run, our self-loathing or lingering guilt (which shows up as asking our kids to forgive us for the same thing over and over again) will damage our children more than the ruptures themselves. "As far as it depends on you . . ." means we confess our sins to God and ask for forgiveness from the kids we've sinned against (Romans 12:18). You cannot control the way your kids respond to an apology. What you do have power over is the model of forgiveness that you provide for them when they apologize to you. Rather than throwing their failures back in their faces, you can use the language of apology: "I forgive you, and I will not hold it against you."

In our house, we outlawed "It's okay" in response to an apology. If my kids say, "It's okay," when I apologize to them, I will say, "Nope, what I did is *not* okay, but it can be *forgiven,* and those are the words I long to hear from you."

The Strengthening Power of Conflict Resolution

Many of us fear that our ruptures are ruining our kids, but child psychologists say it's not the rupture that does the damage; it's the lack of repair. Rupture is inevitable, but it's also not irredeemable. In fact, ruptures provide us with an incredible opportunity. Similarly to the way that micro-ruptures during exercise make muscles stronger, developmental psychologists confirm that when discord is followed by repair, relationships grow stronger—not weaker.[5]

Each time you initiate repair after a rupture with your child, it helps them develop resilience. They learn that good things can follow bad things; they learn that conflict doesn't mean that a relationship is ending; they discover that relationships can be deepened as they are characterized by confession, reconnection, and commitment. That knowledge will be a gift to their future friendships, marriages, and goals as they experience friction or setbacks.

Apply the Gospel When You Remember Your Sin

One of my favorite things about the women's Bible study at my church is that it is divided into intergenerational study groups. I sit around a table talking about God's Word each week with women who have raised their children to adulthood and are now helping to raise their grandchildren.

One day the text was Hebrews 8:12, and my table leader asked, "What difference does it make that God remembers your sin no more?" Women started rattling off stories from their days with young children. "I can remember one time," my table leader began, "when my daughter was about three. She was being so defiant, and I was so frustrated, and it had been such a long morning. After a few times of repeating the same thing, I just whapped her arm with the hairbrush in my hand. And I still think about it all the time."

As my friend Leslie Bennett once said, we can't control our memory banks, but we *can* control the way we respond to what they put before us. First John 1:9 says that "if we confess our sins, he is faithful and just and will forgive us our sins and purify us from all unrighteousness." So when you confess to God, you receive not only his forgiveness but also the gift of a clear conscience. And how arrogant would it be to continue to pronounce yourself condemned when the One with the highest authority has declared you forgiven?

Why am I talking about your forgiveness from God in a chapter about connection and repair with your kids? Because if you do not receive God's forgiveness and agree with him that you are forgiven by forgiving yourself (self-repair), either you'll overidentify with the part of you that committed that sin and therefore repeat or justify it, or you will look elsewhere for the benediction you crave. Either you'll attempt to "make up for" what you did or further burden your children with your need for constant reassurance or your friends with the fishing expedition for "You're a great mom" compliments.

If we are convinced that God remembers our sin no more, then when *we* remember it, we can grieve its effects and even apologize to those who were affected, if we have not already done so. However, we do not need to wallow in guilt or shame. Instead, our grief in remembrance can serve as an occasion to recall and again be amazed by God's grace, springing us up into joy once more.

An Example to Follow

Maybe you are hesitant to humble yourself before your child to apologize because you fear that you will lose their respect or you don't want to highlight your failure. Perhaps you think that if you draw attention to your wrongs, that's what they'll remember or, worse, imitate. However, one of the most important examples you can provide for your kids is how to handle failure. Each time we fail, we are given the opportunity to model repentance and reconciliation.

Sure, it's important that we are reconciled to one another, but the greater need we all have is to be reconciled to God. I will never be a perfect mom. But if my kids can look back and say that their mama was a fast repenter, quick to repair, and committed to growth, I'll take it. And I pray those qualities rub off on them. I hope my children can follow in my frail footsteps straight to our faithful Savior.

Our response to our shortcomings teaches our kids how to respond to their own with gospel humility. And that's the sort of example that, when followed, saves souls and salvages relationships. Repenting in front of our kids and repairing with our kids is a gift to their relationships with God, friends, future spouses, children, coworkers, churches, and also themselves. When they experience conflict, they'll know the path to restoration is humble ownership. When they mess up, they'll know the path to peace is repentance. And hopefully, having experienced a secure attachment to their parent, they'll be set up to have a secure attachment to God.

Parenting Connection

When my kids have conflicts, rather than stepping in as a judge, I try to help them practice reconciliation. To one who has caused an offense, I will usually ask them to look at the face of their sibling or friend and tell me what they are feeling. This trains them to be aware of and hopefully attuned to the feelings of others. "It looks like you might have a relationship that needs repairing," I will say. Then I ask, "Is there anything you might need to say 'I'm sorry' for?" I want the words "I'm sorry" and "I forgive you" to feel super familiar coming off their lips.

When one of them feels as if they have been wronged, we follow a four-step process for conflict resolution. They know they're supposed to first try to work it out before involving me. But if they do come to me, I try to act less like an arbiter of justice and more like a facilitator, guiding them through the steps. "When someone does something we don't like, or tries to take something from us, what should we do?" I ask and hold up four fingers. We walk through the steps together, figuring out what went wrong and trying again.

Here's how you can introduce this method to your kids:

Can you hold up four fingers? I'm going to teach you four steps we're going to use when we have a conflict. Here they are!

1. **Stop! Step Back!**

   When we take our hands off the thing we're fighting over or take a step back from something we disagree about, we communicate that people are more important than things and show that we value the relationship and doing what's right more than having our way.

2. **Use calm, kind words to communicate your feelings or desires.**

   Calm, kind words sound like, "May I please have that . . . ?" or "I don't like how you're playing. Please stop."

3. **Listen to the response of the other person and try to work it out.**

   You are a problem-solver! You can work together to figure out a solution. Maybe you could say, "When you finish, can I have a turn?" Or you could work out a trade or compromise that makes it a good deal for everybody.

4. **If it isn't working, come get an adult.**

   If someone isn't listening, you can fight the temptation to grab, push, hit, or yell to get your way by coming to ask me for help. This is more peaceful and more productive!

Now, can you point to your fingers and tell me the steps?

This method is starting to click in our house. I overhear my kids using this language with each other. Violence is being avoided, and peace is being made in the pursuit of self-control, humility, and love of neighbor. They'll practice it now with toys and turn-taking while they're younger, but as they grow, the principle will hold as their conflicts become more complex.

Believe It for Your Motherhood

You won't parent perfectly—but you can respond to your failures faithfully. When ruptures happen, rest in the finished work of Jesus, which allows you to pause, reflect with honesty, and move from reaction to responsibly. Own what was yours to own, confess it, receive God's forgiveness, and then practice repair with your child. This will not only strengthen your relationship and help them develop resilience but will also give them an example to follow in their own relationships, with God and others.

Be kind and compassionate to one another, forgiving each other, just as in Christ God forgave you.
—Ephesians 4:32

Apply It to Your Parenting

- Invite your kids to pay attention to the faces and emotions of those with whom they have conflict.
- When one of your kids commits a wrong, say, "It looks like you have a relationship to repair," and ask what they might need to say "I'm sorry" for.
- Teach your kids the steps for conflict resolution, viewing every conflict as an opportunity to practice instead of an indication that you're doing something wrong.

Chapter 11

Trusting God with Your Kids

Motherhood is an incredible responsibility. A friend of mine with a child with complex medical needs once lamented the expression "It's not all up to you," saying, "But it *is* all up to me, actually. If I forget his meds, he could die." As moms, we do have a lot of responsibilities. We are to care for our children body and soul, and that task should feel weighty to us. But the weight of that outcome doesn't fall on our shoulders. When it comes to salvation, it is most assuredly not all up to us.

The title of this book appealed to your suspicion that you're having a negative impact on your kids. We've looked at ways to become the most Christlike, faithful mom you can possibly be, but perhaps, as we can conclude this journey together, even as you're encouraged by God's work of transformation, you might still be wondering, "But *am* I ruining them?" Let's address that question head on.

God Is a God of Redemption

The damage I have done to my kids is sometimes obvious, like the time one of my boys was up all night throwing up because I didn't properly wash the eggs from our backyard chickens. Other times it's harder to perceive. Someone once told me that my son was anxious because I was passing anxiety to him through my breastmilk.

The message of this book is not "Don't worry, you're not messing up your kids!" The truth is, because you are not perfect, you have harmed and will continue to harm to your children. You're going to get it wrong. The good news is, which was stated previously but is worth repeating, is that *nothing* is beyond redemption. Negative attachment patterns, implicit memories, generational sin struggles—none of it is outside the scope of what God can redeem. Redemption is his specialty, after all.

And transformation is possible. Repentance and grace lead to real change over time. The beauty of your commitment to gospel transformation is this: As you experience healing and growth, and are filled with hope for your *own* ability to change, your hope for the healing and growth of your *children* will increase as well.

Ultimately, it is confidence in *God's* ability to redeem and to heal that will give you hope for your kids apart from your own performance as a mom. Some of the godliest people I know were raised by some of the worst parents I've ever heard of. One of my most treasured friends grew up with a mom who would disappear for weeks at a time. This friend, who spent her teenage years knocking on hotel room doors in search of her mother, grew up to be a compassionate, emotionally intelligent woman with amazing boundaries. One of the best men I know was beaten by his father and verbally abused by his mother. He is gentle, kind, and empathetic. Both of these people love Jesus with a passion and are laying down their lives for the sake of his kingdom.

My friends aren't the only ones with stories like this. Many of the books I read in preparation for writing this one, authored by counselors, were filled with stories of how their clients had been negatively impacted by explosive, hypercritical, manipulative, detached, absent, or withdrawn parents. These stories terrified me as I considered my impact on my kids. But the only reason those stories were included in these books was that each of them was a story of *transformation*. These adults with imperfect parents were not *ruined*. Each of these people provided an example of becoming aware of the impact of their childhoods and, as a result, experiencing healing and flourishing.

God Can Work Through Your Failures

I love the way a story in Joshua 7 and 8 showcases that God not only works despite our failures but can even use them to accomplish his good purposes. God was the undeniable source of victory for the Israelites at Jericho. Riding this wave of victory, Joshua prepared for battle with Ai. Had he consulted God, Joshua would have learned that because Achan took some of the plunder from Babylonia that was supposed to have been destroyed (Joshua 7:21), God's anger burned against Israel. But Joshua, rather than "weary[ing] the whole army" (Joshua 7:3), arrogantly sent only a handful of fighting men to seize Ai—without asking God for instruction or help. Evidently, they thought the fight was something they could handle in their own strength. When Israel lost the battle, and thirty-six men lost their lives, Joshua accused God of not being faithful. In reality, it was the faithlessness of the people of Israel that led to their defeat. And that defeat exposed their need for God.

Once Joshua dealt with Achan and the devoted things, God told him to take his whole army up to Ai, assuring him that he had given the city into their hands (Joshua 8:1). With the presence of God restored as the source of his courage, Joshua disclosed the battle plan to the Israelites. Israel would pretend to retreat, causing Ai to say, "They are running away from us, *just as they did before,*" (Joshua 8:6, emphasis mine). Then Israel's men were told to "rise up from ambush and take the city," and God would give it into their hand (Joshua 8:7). The battle played out precisely according to plan.

This story puts God's redemptive power on display. The circumstances of Joshua's former self-induced humiliation (running away in retreat) are precisely the means God used to secure his victory (feigning running away in retreat, *just as they did before*). Romans 8:28 assures us that God works *all* things together for the good of those who love him. "All" encompasses the suffering we endure, but it also includes the ways we arrogantly forge ahead in our own strength or act apart from faith. God can use even our mistakes for his glory. When, like Joshua, we are tempted to accuse him of being unfaithful because things aren't going well in parenting, let us remember his character and look to him to cover us, relying more fully on him as our source of courage, strength, and victory.

And when things are going badly and seem to be the direct result of our own foolishness, we can rest assured that God specializes in turning what looks like defeat into victory. Think of Calvary. The greatest human error in history was the precise means through which God rescued creation. Nothing is beyond redemption.

Don't overestimate the negative impact you will have on who your children turn out to be. God will accomplish his purposes in their lives despite your shortcomings. He may even use the ways you have fallen short, consciously or unconsciously, to draw them to himself. God might even accomplish his purposes for their lives *through* your shortcomings! You cannot underestimate God's ability to use your failures for good in your kids' lives. His ability to redeem your children far outweighs your ability to ruin them.

God Can Work Through Your Faithfulness

And if God can work through your failures, he can surely work through your faithfulness. You may not be perfect, but I'm sure there's plenty you're getting right. I recently had a conversation with an incredible young man in our community who just graduated and is headed to join an athletic team at the Naval Academy. He was talking to me about his appreciation for his mama. "Did she ever yell? Lose her temper?" I asked. "Oh," he laughed, "more than you know! But," he added, "she also loved us like crazy and gave raising us her very best effort."

In the introduction to his book *Devoted: Great Men and Their Godly Moms,* Tim Challies writes,

> It may surprise us, though, to learn of how many of our Christian heroes . . . would insist that their primary spiritual influencer had been their mother. One of history's greatest preachers would say with affection, "I'm sure that, in my early youth, no teacher ever made such an impression upon my mind as the instruction of my mother," while one of its most committed evangelists would say, "I learned more about Christianity from my mother than from

> all the theologians in England." . . . A great defender of the faith would write about an overwhelming moment of doubt, then relate how he found deliverance: "My mother [spoke to me] in those dark hours when the lamps burned dim, when I thought that faith was gone and shipwreck had been made of my soul. 'Christ,' she used to say, 'keeps firmer hold on us than we keep on him.'"[1]

The time that you spend reading Bible stories with your kids, praying with them, singing truth over them, repenting to and in front of them, listening to them, being attuned to them, enjoying creation with them, and just living the Christian life in front of them—all of it matters. I know you're afraid of the effects of your failures, but you also need to know that God can use your *faithfulness* in a powerful way in the lives of your children.

Our failures as moms do not render our faithfulness ineffective or nullify God's faithfulness to us or to our kids. Hebrews 11 is often called the "hall of faith." It's like a who's who of the redemptive story, praising the faithfulness of biblical characters whom God used mightily in his story of redemption. Abraham is included in it. So is Sarah. Both of them are praised for their faithfulness, even though Abraham basically pimped out his wife to Pharaoh and Sarah sought to take matters into her own hands by trying to architect her family, asking her husband to sleep with her servant. This is one of the most important sets of parents in redemptive history, and they seriously blew it, but their failures did not negate God's faithfulness or his ability to use them. Despite their failures, he still used their faithfulness to accomplish his redemptive purposes in their family and in his bigger story of redemption.

Relax into the Providence of God

The first Sunday that my son took communion, rather than celebrating in excitement, I cried in fear. As we sang the "prone to wander" line of the hymn "Come, Thou Fount of Every Blessing," I thought about my own struggles with doubt and wondered if his faith would last.

At the core of my fears regarding how my actions will impact my kids is a desire to save them. I want to save them from pain, to rescue them from broken relationships and heartaches, to deliver them from the sorrow of unrealized dreams, and especially to protect them from hell. But friend, you and I both need to get nice and comfy with the fact that we can't save our kids. We weren't designed to. You could never be a good enough mother to save your children. Therefore, your motivation for parenting well, and mine, more than fear, must be faith.

In addition to you seeing the positive impact of ordinary, imperfect mothers on their godly sons and daughters, I want you to hear the final exhortation of that mother in Tim Challies's book to her doubting child: God is the initiator and sustainer of the covenant of salvation.

The work you do as a mom is work that you must carry out by grace through faith in the One who is able to do abundantly more than you could ever ask or imagine (Ephesians 3:20). The apostle Paul knew this too, writing to the church at Corinth, "I planted the seed, Apollos watered it, but God has been making it grow. So neither the one who plants nor the one who waters is anything, but only God, who makes things grow. . . . For we are co-workers in God's service" (1 Corinthians 3:6–7, 9). As moms, we can plant seeds of truth in our kids' hearts, but we cannot make them grow. However, we can entrust our kids to the God who can.

Each time you feel anxiety about the souls of your kids, feeling afraid of either your power to mess things up or your lack of power to ensure a positive outcome, let it be a marker to remember the power of God to save, and relax into his providence.

Father, more than these children are mine, they are yours.

Help me to leave the work of saving them to you, instead of bearing a burden that was never mine. You alone can save. I will be faithful to plant, but only you can give the growth.

God Can Work Through His Church

We can also enlist the help of other people to do the watering. It's clear that Paul sees the need for coworkers. We've already referenced the adage that it takes a village to raise a child. Well, in his church, God has provided you with one. Remember, one of the main shared experiences of kids who continued to attend church after they graduated from high school was not the quality of their moms; it was that kids connected with other adults at church who intentionally invested in them.[2] One study even found significant relationships with adults other than their parents to be a preeminent factor in adolescent faith maturity.[3]

In the mornings, before we go our separate ways, each member of our family briefly answers the question, "How do you need God's help today?" I begin my prayers with, "Father . . . ," the way my daddy did. But each of my boys begins differently: "Our great God and king . . ." "Lord Jesus . . ." "Father God . . ." And I can tell you precisely who from Hilton Head Presbyterian Church they are emulating—pastors, Sunday school teachers, friends who have hosted us for dinner. The adults at our church are shaping the spiritual lives of my kids. Rob Maharrey is the man who teaches the rambunctious boys who make up one of my son's Sunday school classes. That child sometimes blows me away with his knowledge and gospel application, and I'll ask where he learned something. "Mr. Rob taught me," he says.

This Sunday, my youngest sprinted over and jumped into the arms of the elderly gentleman who used to watch him in the nursery. That man once told me that he felt embarrassed that he didn't have more gifts with which to serve—that's why he served in the nursery. With tear-filled eyes, I told him that he was playing one of the most important spiritual roles in the life of my son, teaching him that he is loved within the body of Christ, that these people are his family.

The families we do life with matter too. My kids are watching the marriages of these couples. They're being loved by them and sometimes even challenged by them. I know that as my kids grow, they will sometimes feel more comfortable bringing issues to our friends than to my husband and me.

My dearest friend, who will soon be our next-door neighbor, often comments how thankful she is that I don't have daughters so that I'll have all my girl energy to invest in hers! And I joke that every hug and exchange I have with her little girl is storing up chips to cash in when she's not listening to her mom when she's in high school. Look around at the people God has placed in your kids' lives to love and nurture and guide them. It's not all up to you. You cannot be everything your kids need. You were never meant to be. That's why God brought you into a family. You're not alone.

God Can Work Through Your Prayers

God has given you his people, and he's also given you his Spirit by whom you can cry out to him. We have to depend not on the planting or watering but on God, who gives the growth. You can be faithful to sow seeds of truth. God's people can support your efforts. But only God's Spirit can bring growth. Faith in God expresses itself through prayer. Pray for your kids. Pray with your kids. God works through prayer to accomplish his will. It's the best thing you can do for your children.

God will use your efforts. He will use your failure. He will use your community. He will use your prayers. God is at work in ways that you cannot begin to perceive.

We recently took a kid-free vacation with a few other couples, and I brought an intentional question for the dinner table each night. One of the guys, when asked who had made the greatest impact on his life, positive or negative, answered by saying, "Without a doubt, it's my mom." He continued by saying that she wasn't perfect, but he always knew she was praying for him. During his teen years, when he was making poor choices, or in his words, "being a little punk," he said she never made his struggles about herself. "She didn't try to control the situation or make it about her. She entrusted me to God. And that had a profound impact on me."

Admittedly, even as I have written this book, I constantly battle the desire to be perfect. Under all this effort lies the belief that if I can just get it right—if I can consider everything from every angle and tell all the right stories in all the right places—then this book will make an impact. But the truth is, if this book makes any difference in the life of any mom who reads it, it will be because God did the work supernaturally in the heart of the reader by the power of his Spirit, not because my words were powerful. Just like I could never be a good enough writer to change your heart, you could never be a good enough mother to save your children. But God can use our efforts to accomplish his purposes.

Paul Tripp calls Matthew 28:18–20 "the best parenting passage in the entire Bible" because in it, Jesus says, "All authority in heaven and on earth has been given to me."[4] Tripp continues,

> You do not have to load the burden of your children's welfare on your shoulders every morning. Every day remind yourself of this truth. The welfare of your children does not rest on your shoulders, but on the shoulders of the One who sent you. He has the power to do what you could never do. Unlike us, he is never weak or weary. He never gets lost in his own discouragement or anger. Unlike us, he never looks back and regrets what he has done. He always does what is just, good, wise, kind, loving, gracious, and right. He loves our children more than we ever will—so much so that he died so that they would have everything that they need to be what they're supposed to be and live as they were created to live. Thankfully, the great heavenly Father's shoulders are big enough to carry what our small parenting shoulders could never bear, and he willingly bears the burdens that would otherwise crush and disable us.[5]

God Can Work Through Whatever He Chooses

I inherited a love of growing things from my grandmother. When I was growing up, one of my favorite things to do was walk her property with her as she pointed out plants and told me their names. A few years ago, as I walked my grandmother's property with her, I marveled that so much of the beauty on her property she hadn't planted herself. "Oh, that [whatever kind of plant] just volunteered there," she would say. This phrase simply means that the plant just popped up from scattered seeds that birds had dropped.

I often labor under the falsehood that the success and salvation of my children hinge on my ability to be wise and consistent. Planting and watering are acts of faithfulness for a parent, as is faithfully pruning and tending to the hearts of our children. But God gently reminded me through a volunteer blueberry bush teeming with fruit that all is grace, and he's the one who gives the growth—sometimes *despite* my failure, sometimes *through* my failure, sometimes through my *faithfulness,* and sometimes by means that have *nothing to do with me.*

I want to believe that if I do x, y, and z as a mom, the output will be perfectly obedient and Spirit-filled children who love God's Word and have regenerate hearts. But parenting isn't about results; it's about faithfulness. I've craved credit for the good my kids do since they cracked a smile for the first time as infants. But how beautifully freeing it is to see that God grows fruitful bushes from pooped-out seeds. As much as your good work and efforts in motherhood matter, they are not ultimate. God is able. He will accomplish his purposes in your children's lives no matter what. My prayer is that your role in their growth might be freeing and enjoyable instead of burdensome and terrifying because of your faith in the only One who changes hearts.

God Gets All the Glory

"He's just thinning my army." I often say this to my husband or friends when a task feels beyond me, like when our whole house got the stomach bug right before a deadline for the first draft of this book. The phrase references a story from chapter 7 of the book of Judges in which God asked Gideon to reduce his army from about 32,000 men to a mere 300. Gideon obeyed God, and this tiny army achieved an enormous victory. The thinning of his army and the underdog victory made it abundantly clear that God, not the strength of Gideon's army or the quality of Gideon's leadership, was the source of their win over the Midianites. God loves to put his power and faithfulness on display.

Gideon's story reminds me not to put confidence in my own abilities but instead to depend on God's power and grace. If you feel like you're the wrong person for the job, that you don't know enough, or that you're under-resourced or underqualified, you're in the perfect position to give God glory for the work he accomplishes in the lives of your kids. No amount of good parenting can place your kids beyond the need of God's grace, and no amount of bad parenting will place your kids beyond the reach of God's grace. It will be his grace, not your efforts, that saves them. Let your own shortcomings be a reminder of that very relieving fact. One day, if someone compliments how well your kids turned out and asks what your secret is, I hope you'll be able to say with confidence, "To God be the glory. It was all his grace."

Believe It for Your Motherhood

You could never be a good enough mom to save your kids or make them turn out well. But God is faithful! He can use both your faithfulness and your failures to draw them to himself.

Unless the LORD builds the house,
the builders labor in vain.
—Psalm 127:1

Conclusion

Once, as we were driving somewhere as a family, after a particularly shiny morning for me as a mom, my husband called to the back seat, "Do you boys know that you have the best mom in the whole world?"

"Yeah!" two of them called out enthusiastically.

The six-year-old waited for that enthusiasm to die down before letting out a pensive, persnickety, "Wellll . . ."

"Well, what?" his dad inquired, incredulous.

"I mean," my son continued, "there are a *lot* of moms in the world. It's very possible that there's a better mom out there *somewhere*."

It's been a few years since that car conversation. Thankfully, as I was putting this same child to bed last night, he told me—unsolicited, I might add—that he thinks I am, in fact, the best mom in the world. I giggled, remembering his previous hesitation.

My hyperanalytical six-year-old was right, though; there *are* a lot of moms in the world. And though my husband's superlative was casually issued and was not intended to elicit the true contest that my son's very literal brain immediately began, it did leave me wondering.

As I wrote this book, I often tried to imagine who you might be, what your kids are like, what your own childhood was like, and what life looks like for you. I also imagined the women in my world doing the hard work of motherhood amid some really hard things. I don't know you, and I don't know what comes to mind when you wonder, "Am I ruining my kids?" But I can confidently tell you this: You're the best mom for your kids because you're the mom that God gave them. And he didn't give them to a more perfect version of you; he purposely gave them to a work-in-progress you. Who better to teach them how to run to Christ when they fail than a mom who must do that regularly? How better to teach them the skills of reconciliation than giving them a mom who often has to ask for forgiveness? Who better to show them care and compassion than you, who knows what it is to need it?

You are the mom God chose for your kids, however they came to be in your care, whether through birth, adoption, or fostering. Being a perfect mom is not a prerequisite for being a faithful or fruitful mom. So, the question is, how can you be the most faithful and fruitful mother possible?

An Action Plan

In light of all that you've read, let's make an easy-to-reference action plan for change, shall we? The next time you feel that you're ruining your kids or desire to be a better mom or have a deep sense that you've blown it, here's what you're going to do:

1. **Calm** your nervous system.
2. **Claim** your gospel identity.
3. **Confess** disordered loves.

4. **Consider** your humanity, circumstances, needs, and limits and make necessary changes.
5. Get **curious** about how your actions might reveal unhealed hurts, then practice **compassion** and run to God for comfort.
6. **Connect** with your child again, repairing any rupture that has occurred.
7. **Continue** to embrace God's tools for change: prayer, Scripture, hardship, and community.

An Invitation to Rest

This book gave you a lot of practical suggestions of things to do, but as we conclude, I want to invite you not to get busy but to rest. My parting words to conclude our journey together are an exhortation to keep going in your work as a mom, but not to strive out of a fear of failure or a desire to be better or a need to ensure your kids turn out okay. This is an invitation to rest in the work that has been done for you, is being done in you, and ultimately will be accomplished in, for, and all around you when Christ returns.

Rest in the Finished Work of Jesus

It is rest in this finished work that will give you the courage to be honest about your shortcomings.

It is rest in this finished work that will give you the humility to apologize and be reconciled to your children.

It is rest in this finished work that will give you the security you need to not place the burden of your worth on your kids or their behavior.

Rest in the Ongoing Work of Jesus

It is rest in his ongoing work that will keep you from feeling alone in the task of motherhood, since he is always with you and helping you by his Spirit.

It is rest in his ongoing work in your kids that will help you hold out hope when it feels like there's no fruit from your labor.

Rest in the Ultimate Work of Jesus

When you feel the pain, toil, and hardship of motherhood, look forward to the day of redemption, the final and complete deliverance for God's people from sin and its effects, with anticipation and relief.

When you experience the beauty of motherhood—those moments when you want to freeze time because they hold so much joy that your heart could burst, and you wish it could always be this way—let it be a glimpse into glory, a sign of the coming reality of eternal life, rest, joy, and peace.

It is rest in this coming reality that will give you the endurance to keep going when you feel like quitting.

The greatest irony will be that despite all the ways you've blown it, you'll hear the voice of our Father, as he references the good works you've done as a mother, say, "Well done, good and faithful servant."

I hope you can replace the fearful phrase "Help! I'm ruining my kids!" with the faith-filled anthem "The Lord is my help! I'm filled with hope for my kids."

I know I'm filled with hope when I consider all that he will do in and through *you* in this good work of motherhood, sister.

Peace be with you.

Believe It for Your Motherhood

God is at work.

To him who is able to keep you from stumbling and to present you before his glorious presence without fault and with great joy—to the only God our Savior be glory, majesty, power and authority, through Jesus Christ our Lord, before all ages, now and forevermore! Amen.

—Jude 1:24–25

Acknowledgments

I toyed with the idea of not writing an acknowledgements section, but that wouldn't be fair to my friend Maggie Combs, who took a call from me nearly every time I sat down to, or got up from, writing. Thank you for your gospel encouragement and reassurance through this entire process. This book might not exist without you. I can't believe you're still taking my calls.

To Jenny Royer, thanks for your unwavering love and faith, your consistent encouragement in work and motherhood, and your constant reminder that I don't have some Dollar Tree Holy Spirit.

To Rebecca Joyner and Maggie Yelton—walking alongside you both in motherhood has changed me. I learn so much from your lives and examples. And I don't know where I would be without your friendship.

To my editor Andrea Palpant Dilley, thank you for championing this project, for tiling and retiling this bathroom with me until the structure was exactly right, and for continually urging me to come out from behind the lectern and sit on the sofa with this dear reader. Thanks for loving her. This is a better book—and I'm a better writer and communicator—for your involvement.

And to the entire Zondervan team, thank you for your

commitment to this message. You are all so excellent at what you do, and I'm honored to work with you.

To my agent Don Gates, thank you for your tough love, constant advocacy, and generosity with your experience and wisdom. You made this whole thing happen.

To my executive-ministry-assistant-turned-dear-friend Megan Roberts—your giftedness and dedication behind the scenes freed me up to focus on writing this book. You are a treasure.

To HB—you shepherded me through one of the darkest seasons of my life, and so much of this book was born out of the wrestling you did with me and all that you taught me. Thank you for your commitment to my growth and healing. You are making an incredible difference with your life and work.

To my writer friends and Fight Club girlies—I know, I know, we're not supposed to talk about it—thank you for your solidarity, encouragement, and check-ins, and for your constant reminders to look to the Lord for provision. Bekah Hannah, thanks for making me feel like it was okay to let people actually read this book.

To my Hilton Head PCA family, especially my Focus ladies, thank you for holding me up in prayer and seeing me through this writing process.

To my pastors, thank you, especially Harrison, for the constant reminder that God equips us to do what he asks us to, and Bill, for loaning me essentially your entire library over the last year.

To each of my friends and dear sisters who let me read a section aloud or offered feedback, thank you. Kara Mallory, I'm especially grateful to you for helping me lose words that didn't need to be there.

To my CC Community and fellow tutors, thank you for your constant support in prayer and your godly examples of motherhood.

To my Burn Bootcamp family, especially you, KLang, thank

you for praying for me and for reminding me that book writing happens just like any good workout: one rep at a time.

And to my literal family—David, my closest co-laborer and friend—thank you for every time you sacrificed your (infinitely more fiscally valuable) time to be with our boys so I could meet a deadline. Your affirmation of God's call on my life and support of me using the gifts he's given me mean more than I could possibly convey. I love you, and I'm so grateful not only for the way you support me in the work of Bible teaching and writing, but also for the way you shepherd me in motherhood.

To my three precious sons, thank you for calling this title "silly" from the very beginning, maintaining that it was a preposterous question for me ever to ask of my own motherhood. Thank you, too, for your patience with me. You cheered me on and reminded me (usually without meaning to) what this book is really about. Being your mom is one of the greatest delights of my life. I adore who you are, and I'm so grateful to have a front-row seat as God grows you into the men he made you to be.

To my sisters—I forgive you for "I.H." and the tickling. Thanks for reading portions of this book early on and lending your wisdom, perspective, and encouragement. I love you both.

Mom and Dad, words fail. Thank you for being as committed to getting this book into the world as anyone else, even with all that you've shouldered this year.

And to my faithful Father, who showed his love for me in Christ Jesus—I would be lost without you. To you who are able to do immeasurably more than all I could ask or imagine, according to your power at work within me—to you be the glory in the church and in Christ Jesus throughout all generations, forever and ever. Amen. (Ephesians 3:20–21)

Notes

Chapter 1: Exchanging Shame for a Gospel Identity

1. Edward T. Welch, *Shame Interrupted: How God Lifts the Pain of Worthlessness and Rejection* (New Growth Press, 2012), 28.
2. Welch, *Shame Interrupted*, 2.
3. I've heard this articulation of the gospel from loads of Bible teachers but want to acknowledge that it originated with Jack Miller and Tim Keller.
4. Henri J. M. Nouwen, *Life of the Beloved: Spiritual Living in a Secular World* (Crossroad, 1992), 34.
5. We've used this phrase for a long time based on what my campus minister used to say to open our RUF large group gatherings. My friend Justin Earley talks about doing this in his book *Habits of the Household* (Zondervan, 2021), and I've also seen it in the children's book by Sarah Reju called *Coop Messes Up* (New Growth Press, 2020). I've since seen a lot of other people use some variation of the same refrain, but I'm not sure if it's attributable to anyone.

Chapter 2: Living Within Your Limits

1. Matt Boswell and Matt Papa, "His Mercy Is More," 2016, Getty Music, recorded by Matt Papa and Matt Boswell on *His Mercy Is More: The Hymns of Matt Boswell and Matt Papa* (Getty Music, 2019), digital.

2. Kelly M. Kapic, *You're Only Human: How Your Limits Reflect God's Design and Why That's Good News* (Brazos Press, 2022), 43.
3. Just a note to say, there's more to come on the need for and the mechanics of repair in part 3.
4. James W. Moore, "What Is the Sense of Agency and Why Does It Matter?," *Frontiers in Psychology* 7 (August 29, 2016): 1272, https://doi.org/10.3389/fpsyg.2016.01272; American Psychological Association, "Agency," *APA Dictionary of Psychology*, accessed August 28, 2025, https://dictionary.apa.org/agency.
5. Dan Siegel, "Healthy Mind Platter," Dr. Dan Siegel: Inspire to Rewire, accessed June 6, 2024, https://drdansiegel.com/healthy-mind-platter/.
6. Eating at a deficit is not wrong, but it may be valuable to talk to a nutritionist as you pursue a certain body composition for health's sake to ensure your macro percentages, calorie target, and goal for pace of body fat loss are appropriate for your body and season.
7. Westminster Larger Catechism, Q. 129, The Westminster Standard, accessed June 24, 2025, https://thewestminsterstandard.org/westminster-larger-catechism/#129.

Chapter 3: Looking Beneath the Surface

1. I am not a psychotherapist, a certified biblical counselor, or a medical professional. I'm just a mom, who after much struggling, reading, research, and querying of people who fall into those categories, have developed the convictions that you'll find within this chapter. I know this discussion is super nuanced, but I'm willing to wade into these waters because I believe these are conversations moms need to be having.
2. Edward T. Welch, *Blame It on the Brain: Distinguishing Chemical Imbalances, Brain Disorders, and Disobedience* (P&R Publishing, 1998). I consulted this work to aid my understanding of how the heart and the body relate to each other. I commend it to you for further exploration of this topic.
3. If you wrestle with anxiety, panic attacks, or intrusive thoughts,

I highly recommend picking up a copy of Blair Linne's *Made to Tremble: How Anxiety Became the Best Thing That Ever Happened to My Faith* (B&H Books, 2025). She handles these topics with care and candor.

4. Michael R. Emlet, *Descriptions and Prescriptions: A Biblical Perspective on Psychiatric Diagnoses and Medications* (New Growth Press, 2017). I consulted this work to aid my understanding of the complexities of psychiatric labels and psychotropic medications from a biblical perspective. I found it immensely helpful and commend it to you for further exploration of this topic.
5. I've heard Sissy Goff and David Thomas articulate a similar sentiment about parents who struggle with anxiety. Check out Sissy's book *The Worry-Free Parent* (Bethany House, 2023) for more practical encouragement in this area.

Chapter 4: Engaging Your Story

1. Paul Tautges, *Remade: Embracing Your Complete Identity in Christ* (P&R Publishing, 2016). This devotional-style read was so instrumental in helping my heart understand and embrace my threefold identity as sinner, saint, and sufferer.
2. Alison Cook and Kimberly Miller, *Boundaries for Your Soul: How to Turn Your Overwhelming Thoughts and Feelings into Your Greatest Allies* (Thomas Nelson, 2018). This book aided in my understanding of parts therapy or internal family systems from a biblical worldview.
3. Corrie ten Boom, *The Hiding Place* (Chosen Books, 2006), 42.
4. Annie Wright, "What Is the Window of Tolerance, and Why Is It So Important?," *Psychology Today*, May 23, 2022, https://www.psychologytoday.com/us/blog/making-the-whole-beautiful/202205/what-is-the-window-of-tolerance-and-why-is-it-so-important.
5. Aundi Kolber, *Try Softer: Mindful Parenting for a Joyful Home* (WaterBrook, 2020), 78. I learned most of what I now know about the window of tolerance from Aundi Kolber. Aundi does a beautiful

job of exploring in this book what this chapter merely scratches the surface of. If you'd like to delve deeper into this topic, *Try Softer* is a great place to start.

6. I'm not sure whom this expression is attributable to, but the expression was first introduced to me in a private counseling session with a licensed therapist.
7. Daniel J. Siegel and Tina Payne Bryson, *The Whole-Brain Child: 12 Revolutionary Strategies to Nurture Your Child's Developing Mind* (Delacorte Press, 2011), 121.
8. Kolber, *Try Softer*, 80.
9. I didn't coin this phrase of distinction but have heard its use widely and am not sure to whom it is attributable.
10. For more on the science of breathing and its relationship to our brains, nervous systems, and choices, check out this video of a neuroscientist's explanation: Yewande Pearce, "How to Breathe Correctly to Reduce Stress," YouTube video, 4:55, posted by Headspace, September 17, 2024, https://www.youtube.com/watch?v=2HojLhKlJto.
11. Bessel van der Kolk, *The Body Keeps the Score: Brain, Mind, and Body in the Healing of Trauma* (Penguin Books, 2015), 99.
12. David Powlison, *Good and Angry: Redeeming Anger, Irritation, Complaining, and Bitterness* (New Growth Press, 2016). This book was invaluable as I learned to understand anger as a secondary emotion.
13. Curt Thompson, *The Anatomy of the Soul: Surprising Connections Between Neuroscience and Spiritual Practices That Can Transform Your Life* (Tyndale Momentum, 2010), chap. 8. From this chapter, I gained an understanding of the transformative power of "feeling felt" by God.
14. Peter Scazzero, *Emotionally Healthy Spirituality: It's Impossible to Be Spiritually Mature, While Remaining Emotionally Immature* (Zondervan, 2014), 24.
15. David Thomas, *Raising Emotionally Strong Boys: Tools Your Son Can Build On for Life* (Bethany House, 2022). This book has been

invaluable to me in learning how to teach emotional regulation skills to my three boys.

Chapter 5: Deciding What Needs to Change

1. Justin Taylor, "Why Does Water Come Out of the Water Bottle When It Is Shaken?," The Gospel Coalition, video, posted May 13, 2016, https://www.thegospelcoalition.org/blogs/justin-taylor/why-does-water-come-out-of-the-water-bottle-when-it-is-shaken/.
2. Taylor, "Why Does Water Come Out of the Water Bottle?"
3. Paul David Tripp and Timothy Lane, *How People Change*, 3rd ed. (Crossway, 2019), 16.
4. Thomas Chalmers, *The Expulsive Power of a New Affection*, ed. and abridged by Carolyn Nystrom (Crossway, 2021).
5. We're going to deal with how to repair broken relationships and deal with the consequences of sinful actions in part 3, but for now, our focus is on what will lead to the lasting change we long for.

Chapter 6: Abiding in Christ (Prayer and Scripture)

1. Michael J. Kruger, *Hebrews for You* (The Good Book Company, 2021), 63.
2. For more help with how to study the Bible, I highly recommend the books *Dig Deeper: Tools for Understanding God's Word* by Nigel Benyon and Andrew Sack and *Women of the Word* by Jen Wilkin. Both will equip you with tools that will help you get the most out of reading the Bible.

Chapter 7: Sharing Life with Others (Community)

1. J. R. R. Tolkien, *The Return of the King*, part 3 of *The Lord of the Rings* (Del Rey/Ballantine Books, 2018), book VI, chap. 3, "Mount Doom," 233.
2. Dietrich Bonhoeffer, *Life Together*, trans. John W. Doberstein (Harper & Row, 1954). For more on how to cultivate community, I cannot recommend this book from Dietrich Bonhoeffer enough.

3. Curt Thompson, *The Anatomy of the Soul: Surprising Connections Between Neuroscience and Spiritual Practices That Can Transform Your Life* (Tyndale Momentum, 2010), 137.
4. "Top 5 Predictors of Young People Staying in Church," *Shelby Systems Blog*, May 22, 2017, https://www.shelbysystems.com/blog/top-5-predictors-young-people-staying-church/.

Chapter 8: Enduring Life's Difficulties (Hardship)

1. Paul David Tripp and Timothy Lane, *How People Change*, 3rd ed. (Wheaton, IL: Crossway, 2019). I picked up referring to suffering this way from this book. It's a great place to further explore this concept of transformation through trial.
2. Jonathan Haidt, *The Happiness Hypothesis: Putting Ancient Wisdom and Philosophy to the Test of Modern Science* (Arrow Books, 2006), 145, quoted in Timothy Keller, *Walking with God Through Pain and Suffering* (Riverhead Books, 2013), 166.
3. The Westminster Shorter Catechism, Q.1, in The Westminster Standard, accessed October 26, 2025, https://thewestminsterstandard.org/westminster-shorter-catechism/.
4. Timothy Keller, *Walking with God through Pain and Suffering* (Riverhead Books, 2013), 168.
5. This concept of being created for glory and looking to receive the glory for which we were designed from God alone is something that I learned from hearing the discipleship and evangelism teachings of pastor Randy Pope.
6. Jerry Bridges, *The Discipline of Grace: God's Role and Our Role in the Pursuit of Holiness* (NavPress, 2006), 238.
7. This understanding came as a result of listening to live teaching at a parenting conference from Daystar counselors David Thomas and Sissy Goff. I highly recommend their resources and tools, especially their podcast, *Raising Boys and Girls*.

Chapter 9: Embracing the Process

1. "The Good Part," track 2 on AJR, *The Click*, AJR Productions, 2021.

2. Jeremy Pierre, "Perfectionism Will Only Make You Miserable," Southern Equip, August 20, 2021, https://equip.sbts.edu/article/perfectionism-will-only-make-you-miserable/.
3. Pierre, "Perfectionism Will Only Make You Miserable."
4. Glenn Boozan, *There Are Moms Way Worse Than You: Irrefutable Proof That You Are Indeed a Fantastic Parent*, illustrated by Priscilla Witte (Workman Publishing, 2022).
5. Mathieu Stern, "Yoann Bourgeois Captivates Audience with Powerful Performance About Life (Original Video)," YouTube video, 1:37, posted October 31, 2022, https://www.youtube.com/watch?v=x_DA3dgRSrw.
6. Robert Thune and Will Walker, *The Gospel-Centered Life Study Guide with Leader's Notes* (New Growth Press, 2011), 13.
7. Jackie Hill Perry, video clip from Passion 2025, Instagram video, 1:06, posted by @jackiehillperry via @passion268, August 30, 2025, https://www.instagram.com/p/DGMFgobSrBp/.
8. This story and specific instructions can be found in Joshua 4:1–3.

Chapter 10: Practicing Repair

1. Daniel J. Siegel and Mary Hartzell, *Parenting from the Inside Out: How a Deeper Self-Understanding Can Help You Raise Children Who Thrive* (Tarcher, 2013), 213–14.
2. Siegel and Hartzell, *Parenting from the Inside Out*, 222.
3. Siegel and Hartzell, *Parenting from the Inside Out*, 222.
4. Kaytee Gillis, "Why Child Trauma Survivors Often Blame Themselves," *Psychology Today*, November 6, 2024, https://www.psychologytoday.com/us/blog/invisible-bruises/202411/why-child-trauma-survivors-often-blame-themselves.
5. Aliza Pressman, *The 5 Principles of Parenting: Your Essential Guide to Raising Good Humans* (Gallery Books, 2024), 28.

Chapter 11: Trusting God with Your Kids

1. Tim Challies, *Devoted: Godly Men and Their Godly Moms* (Cruciform Press, 2018), 5–6.

2. "Top 5 Predictors of Young People Staying in Church," *Shelby Systems Blog.*
3. Karen Choi, *Significant Predictors of Adolescents' Faith Maturity* (Association of Youth Ministry Educators, 2014), 16, https://www.aymeducators.org/wp-content/uploads/Significant-Predictors-of-Adolescents-Faith-Maturity-by-Karen-Choi.pdf.
4. Paul David Tripp, *Parenting: 14 Gospel Principles That Can Radically Change Your Family* (Crossway, 2016), 182.
5. Tripp, *Parenting,* 191.

Group Discussion Guide

Introduction: Desperate for Change

Icebreaker: Tell the group a little about yourself and your family.

1. What about the title of this book appealed to you?
2. In what way is motherhood not what you expected? In what way are you not the mom you thought you'd be?
3. How would you finish this sentence: I would be a better mom if I had more . . .?
4. Can you relate at all to the dashboard/puppy story? If you're willing, share a time you felt similarly.
5. What else from the introduction stood out to you? Is there anything you'd like to talk more about?

Chapter 1: Exchanging Shame for a Gospel Identity

Icebreaker: What is your favorite thing to wear right now?

1. Can you remember your earliest or perhaps your most vivid realization that motherhood wasn't what you expected it to be? Or that you were not the mom you thought or hoped you'd be?
2. What words or phrases from the section on shame resonate with you?

3. What are some of the "fig leaves" you reach for to cover yourself when you don't feel like a "good mom"?
4. What box from the orphan chart most clearly resembled your mentality as a mom?
5. What stood out from the Parenting Connection in this chapter?

Chapter 2: **Living Within Your Limits**

Icebreaker: If your week this week had a theme song, what would it be?

1. Which item on the Healthy Mind Platter feels like the most challenging one for you this season?
2. What are your specific limits right now, both personal and seasonal or circumstantial? Which of them are you most tempted to ignore?
3. In light of what you've read, is there any change you feel compelled to make?
4. Read 2 Corinthians 12:9 out loud together. Have each willing member of the group share what word in this verse most stands out to them and why.
5. What stood out from the Parenting Connection in this chapter?

Chapter 3: **Looking Beneath the Surface**

Icebreaker: If you had a famous moms costume party, who would you dress up as?

1. Which "ditch" do you find yourself leaning toward? Are you more likely to address your sinful flesh or your broken mind/body? How did this chapter speak to your tendency?
2. If anyone is willing to share, discuss some of the current ways

that members of the group have or are currently experiencing physical or psychological challenges.

3. Does anyone in the group know of examples, either from themselves or from someone they know, in which pursuing bodily care or medical assistance has aided in the struggle against sinful behavior?
4. What portion of this chapter felt most encouraging, challenging, or impactful?
5. What stood out from the Parenting Connection in this chapter?

Chapter 4: **Engaging Your Story**

Icebreaker: Which item in the bag you brought best represents this season of your life? (It could also be something that's missing.)

1. Take a few minutes for each member of the group to make a brief timeline of their life, highlighting major events. Invite a few members to share.
2. Share any connections you made between your story (wounds and gaps) and your experience of motherhood.
3. Which of these tools feels most challenging for you to implement? Or which are you most compelled to implement? Are there any that you're already using well?
4. What are you currently facing that might be affecting your own window of tolerance? How might this chapter help or encourage you in that struggle?
5. What stood out from the Parenting Connection in this chapter?

Chapter 5: **Deciding What Needs to Change**

Icebreaker: Share a story of a funny thing your kids have said.

1. After reading this chapter, in which areas are you most hopeful to see change in your own heart and life as a mom?
2. As you read, were you able to make any connections between your behavior and the internal workings of your heart (if helpful, refer to the behavior and root desire chart)? Share if you're willing.
3. What "if only . . ." phrase tempts you to focus on trying to change your circumstances rather than focusing on your heart?
4. How do you typically respond to your own failure? How might following the action plan make a difference? Consider how you might encourage one another to implement these steps the next time you blow it.
5. What stood out from the Parenting Connection in this chapter?

Chapter 6: Abiding In Christ (Prayer and Scripture)

Icebreaker: What was your favorite snack as a kid? What are your kids' favorite snacks to eat right now?

1. What does your prayer life currently look like? How about your relationship to the Bible?
2. Have willing group members share their experiences of prayer or Scripture making a difference in their lives. Invite them to consider the difference these disciplines might make in their current parenting or personal struggles.
3. Read John 15:4 aloud together. Have each willing group member share what word stands out most to them and why.
4. Challenge your group to have a daily dedicated prayer time and spend at least three to five minutes in the Word each day between now and the next time you gather. Ask each person to share a goal for when and how they'll do that (you can send

one another encouragement or pictures throughout the week if that helps!).

5. What stood out to you from the Parenting Connection in this chapter?

Chapter 7: Sharing Life with Others (Community)

Icebreaker: Who in your life would you say has had the greatest impact on your life and why?

1. What is your relationship with the local church like (historically and currently)? How have you felt supported or disappointed?
2. Have each group member share about their own current community. Do you have people in your life who remind you of grace and challenge you? Or simply relate and commiserate? How might you foster these types of relationships?
3. What older women in your life do you admire or look up to? How might you invite them to share their life and wisdom with you?
4. How do you feel about the word *accountability*? Is it something that you tend to welcome or avoid?
5. What stood out to you from the Parenting Connection in this chapter?

Chapter 8: Enduring Life's Difficulties (Hardship)

Icebreaker: Tell us something one of your kids did that delighted or surprised you (in a good way) this week.

1. Have you found yourself seeking satisfaction from motherhood? What might be a helpful indicator of when that is happening?
2. Anyone who is willing or able to share, tell us about a time that suffering either clarified your purpose, helped you rely more on God, or resulted in spiritual maturity?

3. Think of the last hard thing you experienced, big or small. How did you respond? What might it have looked like to "endure it as discipline"?
4. Read Romans 5:3–5 aloud together. Have each willing group member share what verse stands out to them the most and why.
5. What stood out to you from the Parenting Connection in this chapter?

Chapter 9: **Embracing the Process**

Icebreaker: Share a skill that you have that you had to learn or acquire.

1. What distracts you most from your pursuit of holiness for the glory of God: concern with perfectionism, progress, the opinions of others?
2. Who (or what type of mom) do you tend to compare yourself to in motherhood? How was this chapter an encouragement to you, whether in envy or pride?
3. Let's take a moment to see and celebrate change in our own lives or in the lives of the other members of this group? How do you see God at work in you? In the other women here?
4. How does seeing yourself as a person in process change your experience of motherhood? What particular truths from this chapter are you personally needing to cling to?
5. What stood out to you from the Parenting Connection in this chapter?

Chapter 10: **Practicing Repair**

Icebreaker: What's one thing your kids might be surprised to learn about you?

1. Did you grow up in a house where people apologized to one another? How has that impacted you as a mom?
2. Have you ever taken time to reflect like this after a rupture with your kids? What do you typically do? How might these steps transform your experience?
3. How did this chapter impact your view of conflict and ruptures with your kids?
4. Do you struggle to forgive yourself? How might the gospel transform your experience of your failure and your kids' experience of you?
5. What stood out to you from the Parenting Connection in this chapter?

Chapter 11: Trusting God with Your Kids

Icebreaker: Share about a recent time that you either tripped, fell, or failed (not like a moral failure . . . just a goofy one).

1. What aspects of motherhood reinforce the feeling that it's all up to you? How might this way of thinking have a negative spiritual impact on your motherhood?
2. How does it feel to read that you will inevitably negatively impact your children? Relieving? Defeating?
3. Do you have faith in God's ability to work through your failures? What about your faithfulness? Which is harder for you to embrace?
4. What is your involvement in the local church like? Are your kids known there? How are you inviting others to do the work of watering in your kids' lives?
5. What stood out to you from the Parenting Connection in this chapter?

Conclusion

1. Is there anything that stood out to you or resonated with you from the conclusion that you'd like to talk more about?
2. Think back on the first time that this group met together. How have you seen God work in your life since then?
3. What are you hopeful for as we conclude our time together?